Turning

The Magic and Mystery
of More Days

 MASCOT
BOOKS
an imprint of Amplify Publishing Group

www.mascotbooks.com

Turning: The Magic and Mystery of More Days

For more information, please contact:
Mascot Books, an imprint of Amplify Publishing Group
620 Herndon Parkway, Suite 320
Herndon, VA 20170
info@mascotbooks.com

Library of Congress Control Number: 2021922801

CPSIA Code: PRV0422A
ISBN-13: 978-1-63755-055-7

Printed in the United States

To all those who
turn these pages:

May your senses
sharpen
to
the magic
and mysteries
that come near
to you

and make all things new.

—Becky

Turning

The Magic and Mystery
of More Days

Becky Blue, RN, MS

Contents

Introduction

I was on maternity leave with our third child in the winter of 1994 when I bundled up baby Elliot and headed over to the senior citizen center in the small town of Luverne, Minnesota. I can still picture the gathering space filled with probably seventy-five older adults, all seated with their coffee and ready to learn from their guest speaker—me. A few months prior, they had requested the geriatric clinical nurse specialist give a talk about "Sexuality and Aging." I was thirty-four years old and, for whatever reason, fully confident that I could speak on this topic, so I did.

Now, as I approach my sixtieth birthday and what I like to call my "third act" of life, that day twenty-five years ago makes me laugh, cringe, and want to apologize to the sweet folks who had to listen to some upstart nurse whose main concern was if her milk was going to leak in the middle of her presentation.

(Please, Elliot, don't start crying!) That was my career at the beginning of my "second act."

I spent most of my thirties educating older adults about what happens to people as they age. I talked about how their sense of smell changes, how they should prevent falls, how to remember to take their medications, and certainly how not to be depressed about it all. Now, I'm realizing that I was the student, and they were the teachers.

My next gig as a nurse was in the world of faith community nursing—a perfect environment for Jesus-loving, church-nerd me. It required building relationships with nurses and volunteers and looking at clients as whole beings—body, mind, and spirit. I worked with the most empathetic nurses I have ever encountered, many of whom were approaching or had past their sixtieth birthdays and still giving, giving, giving.

After retiring a couple of years ago (well, you never *really* retire from being a nurse), I reached back to a passion from my middle- and high-school days—writing. I'm sure I would have become a writer or journalist had my mom (a high school English teacher) not become ill with breast cancer during my teenage years. Her death when I was sixteen rocked my world. I have often said that experiencing a loss of that magnitude can make or break you; fortunately, her death inspired me to become a nurse and launch my career.

I have already outlived my mom. My paranoia about dying at age fifty-six, as she did, has long passed. It is time for my third act, of which she was robbed. It is time for me to finally be the expert on aging because I'm doing it in real time.

Will you join me?

Hopefully, you can find inspiration as I shuffle my geriatric nursing experience with my faith life and words of wisdom from some of my favorite sources. Ideally, we will collaborate. Whether you're in your first, second, or third act of life, the gift of more days should suggest delight and surprise—a certain magic. Some of us will recall being children of the 1960s and ask what we want our sixties and seventies to look like. We may end up with more questions than answers around the mystery of reaching a ripe old age. The dialogue will be rich and refreshing.

Feel free to write in the margins; some of my best-loved books are cluttered with pencil marks and notes. You may want to read the book with a friend or family member—someone of similar age or from a different generation—because sharing your personal stories and attitudes about aging can be a priceless gift. Consider *Turning* for a book club or Bible study group. There are suggestions for group study in the back of the book.

You're not alone in anticipating the magic and mystery of more days—unless you want to be. Stick with me for the next ten pages, or maybe even ten chapters or ten years. Together, we'll turn this next page of our lives curiously, boldly, and authentically.

"For the ear tests words as the tongue tastes food.
Let us discern for ourselves what is right; let us learn
together what is good."
Job 34: 3-4

A Time for Everything

There is a time for everything,
And a season for every activity under the heavens:
a time to be born, a time to die,
a time to plant, and time to uproot,
a time to kill, and a time to heal,
a time to tear down and a time to build,
a time to weep and a time to laugh,
a time to mourn and a time to dance,
a time to scatter stones and a time to gather them,
a time to embrace and a time to refrain,
a time to search and a time to give up,
a time to keep and a time to throw away,
a time to tear and a time to mend,
a time to be silent and a time to speak,
a time to love and a time to hate,
a time to war and a time for peace.
Ecclesiastes 3:1-8

Chapter One

Let's Begin Together

"Every person who dared to live the life she dreamed
started by learning the explosive force of God's
lessons. Her soul was liberated from its prison, and life
began to have genuine meaning."

Lucy Swindoll

If mornings when you were eight years old consisted of Tang
orange drink or a Great Shake, we may have had similar child-
hoods. My siblings—two older sisters, Patty and Cindy, and one
younger brother, Paul—and I were heavily influenced by TV
advertisements for any new convenience food, and my mom
was happy to oblige our requests whenever the products were
spotted at Ben's Market in my hometown of Hurley, South

Dakota. Tang went with the astronauts to the moon; what's not to love about that? Great Shakes made you just as cool as the kids dancing on TV with their Great Shakes shakers. And don't even get me started on the cardboard records by cartoon pop band The Archies, which we would carefully cut out of Alpha-Bits cereal boxes.

Life was sweet in 1968.

I loved the music of that decade and still do, but I have to give credit to my sister, Patty, who was six years older and had a radio. My brain still retains all the words to the solid-gold hits of the '60s. One of my favorites is "Turn! Turn! Turn!" written by folk singer Pete Seeger[1] and recorded by The Byrds in 1965, and later by The Seekers (any "Georgy Girl" fans?) and Judy Collins ("Send in the Clowns")—all personal favorites. I was happy to discover that Seeger wrote the song in 1959, the year I was born. My favorite version can be found on YouTube in a classic 1966 video by The Seekers.[2] They're singing in an Australian vineyard while picking grapes. Look it up; it will make your day.

I always thought it was cool that the words for this song came from the Old Testament book of Ecclesiastes. The words are nearly verbatim, with writer Seeger adding the repeating "turn, turn, turn" and a final, hopeful line: "I swear it's not too late." Take a moment to read through the words from Ecclesiastes quoted above or play the song on your phone and sing along.

Is there any portion of life the words of these verses don't describe? At first glance, they are practical lessons—"It is what it is!" as my dad, Juel, a pragmatic farmer, used to say. You may even read the words "one turn forward, one turn back" as pessimistic. How does one get anywhere in this life?

Throughout this book we will be observing turns of our own. The turns we take with our feet, our heads, our hands, our ears, our voices, and our hearts. What causes them to turn? When and where should we turn? When will it be our turn?

This scripture also mentions time as if there is an abundance of it—and maybe there is. As we make our next turn around the sun, do we really believe there is time for every purpose under heaven? Okay, that took a serious turn. Take a moment for a glass of wine (or Tang!) and a few deep breaths. I'd like to share the hope and promises I hear in Ecclesiastes.

First, let me ask if you see yourself as a person of faith—remember, I asked you to stick with me for at least ten pages. I suspect you are a little curious about aging, and we'll definitely address that topic. I know that you are a whole person—you have a body (you look great today!), a mind (don't worry, no quizzes here), and, most importantly, a spirit (think heart and soul, like that classic ditty you taught yourself to play on the piano).

My favorite way to define spirit is by asking the question, "What is your heart pinned to?" The answer can't be "nothing" because everyone's heart is pinned to *something*. It might be Jesus or a different higher being in your personal faith tradition, but it may also be your family, job, food, shopping, or an unending grief. I truly believe we are all a mixed bag of body, mind, and spirit stuff, and our natural tendency is to weigh it all on our birthdays.

My own mixed bag feels somehow lighter when I consider

the commentary on Ecclesiastes 3 from theologian Martin Luther. As a teacher and pastor, Luther inspired a reformation over 500 years ago, and his plain way of speaking about God's Word is still useful today. He hears in Ecclesiastes not to turn to yesterday or tomorrow, but rather to enjoy the present things. Luther asks wisely, "How can someone who is uncertain about the future determine something about the future?" [3]

I can honestly say I am feeling uncertain about my next decade. Will I continue to be healthy? How much help will my children need? Should I start a new career? What will life be like when my husband and I are free to spend much more time together? I hope I'll still like him enough for that whole "time for embracing" thing.

My dad gave me great parting words from his hospital bed ten years ago (I'm sure he didn't realize at the time that they would be the last words he would say to me): "Don't take life too seriously." At that moment, the time to laugh and time to weep intersected. I treasure those words and repeat them often to myself and to my children. Luther put it this way, "Joy has its appointed time. Let us not torment ourselves about future things but enjoy present things." [4]

So, with the music of Pete Seeger in one ear and the words of Ecclesiastes in the other, let's do this together. If there truly is a time for every purpose under heaven, then that time is now.

Let's not take life too seriously.

Your Turn

1. In each of the lines of the Ecclesiastes scripture, underline the word that describes you today. For example: A time to mourn, and a time to dance. Look back at what you've highlighted and reflect. Is today a mourning day for you or a dancing day?

2. What is your heart "pinned" to today? Ponder these words from the Gospel of Matthew, Chapter 6, verse 21 to better understand this concept: "For where your treasure is, there your heart will be also." Have your "treasure" or your "pins" changed over the past month? Year? Write down these different pins and see if you notice any patterns.

3. How has your mixed bag of body, mind, and spirit changed compared to ten years ago? How would you like it to look ten years from now? Write a thank-you note to yourself from the perspective of your older self. What will an older you be grateful for? What choices will you be glad you made?

Chapter Two

Where Did You Learn to Age?

"My grandmother started walking five miles a day
when she was sixty. She's ninety-seven now, and we
don't know where the heck she is."
Ellen DeGeneres

My mom gave birth to me when she was forty years old; consequently, my grandparents and great aunts and uncles were elderly during my formative years. In fact, no matter how old they were, they always looked eighty-five to me! I was always willing to visit them and respectfully listen to their stories and devour their cookies.

Grandma Johnson served us Archway cookies that she kept stored in her oven. Grandma Trumm served fragile homemade sugar cookies with teeny half-filled glasses of Hires Root Beer. I didn't realize how impactful these moments were until later, when I was taught a new way to express myself.

My English teacher during my senior year was Mrs. Gulbranson. She was hired to take over my mom's position at our high school. She taught a creative writing course that gave me a powerful tool—poetry. For that, I will always be grateful to her. In 1978, I penned the following:

Afternoon with Grandma
Not bothering to knock
I catch Grandma in her grubbies
Scarf around her head
Scarf around her neck
Pretty chic for 84 ... 85 ... 86
Monday = wash day
Archie Bunker at 2:30
Lunch at 3
Orange drink and apologized-for-boughten
ginger snaps
"Someday I'll make some cookies."
Warm conversation:
Mrs. Friman's birthday party ... weather ...
Uncle Earl's bad leg ... weather ... trouble in
The Mideast ... weather
"Home is the best place for me."

I'm glad I know
Where to
Find her.

If I were to ask my older cousins, they would recall this same grandma in her sixties and seventies, in the kitchen on the farm, gingham apron on, baking fresh bread for the corn-picking crew, all while corralling her grandchildren. What I know for sure is that no matter what age she was, whenever I walked into her house, she motioned me to come close to her—her vision failing. She would turn her head toward me, gently touch my hand, and touch the fabric of my blouse or dress, commenting, "Oh, you look so pretty today, Becky."

A year later, I wrote the follow-up poem after visiting my grandma in the nursing home. The cadence of the two poems repeats the rhythm of "Turn, Turn, Turn."

Afternoon with Grandma: One Year Later
I find Grandma in her wheelchair
Tied in tight so
"She won't run away from us."
Head hanging in a drowsy stare
At the cold tile floor.
Sunday = visitors
She remembers my name
We sit on the sun porch
"I wish I had lunch for you folks.
They won't let me cook here."

Quiet conversation:
Who was in church ... weather ...
Uncle Earl's corn crop ... weather ...
The new great-grandchild ... weather
"I wish we were back home."
I'm glad I know where to
Find her.

Is it any wonder I chose to be a geriatric nurse?

There are bright days, and there are dark days; more importantly, though, there are *more days*. My role models for aging taught me quiet peace with a hint of wishfulness. My grandparents were accepting and hopeful.

I still clearly remember attending the funeral of a distant cousin who tragically died in his forties. His mother—probably in her seventies—was greeting family after the service, and she told me, "I'm just going to pull myself up by my bootstraps."

These were my people. Strong and independent. Gentle and kind. I likely take those qualities for granted in myself, but I see them in my children, and I am grateful. It reminds me of one of God's great promises written in Matthew 7:17: "A good tree bears good fruit." The days pass quickly, and the tree grows deep roots and long branches. A time to plant, a time to reap.

The exciting opportunity that lies before us is that, for the most part, we can choose how we age. Your role models may have been very different from those I wrote about in my poetry. My geriatric nursing practice was filled with people who made good choices, yet their genetics or circumstances pushed them more toward sickness than health. Nevertheless, many did not let their aging be defined by their list of chronic illnesses. Their identity was measured in time spent with their families or their ability to plant their own garden. They practiced what Pastor Charlotte Gambill preached: "Your infirmity is not your identity."[1]

Like me, you may catch yourself watching for new and inspiring role models. I recently spent some time in airports (pre-pandemic) and couldn't help but take mental notes on which traveler I wanted to be in a few years. It was easy to be enamored by the thin, tanned seventy-something woman with the classic gray ponytail and hiking boots. She appeared to be traveling alone as she walked confidently to her gate with enviable breeziness.

Then there was the couple I chose to pass by because their gait was slower than mine. They clasped each other's hands for balance, and their faces were turned to each other in quiet conversation. The workers at the ticket counters, many of whom appeared to be in their sixties or seventies, caught my eye as they answered the couple's questions with patience and kindness. It's an important exercise to watch those around you and see how they are making their way through their third act.

I'd be remiss if I didn't uplift my Grandpa Johnson here. One of my most valuable life lessons came from him. Grandpa loved his car—a 1966 silver-blue Ford Galaxy 500 that barely fit into the little one-car garage attached to their yellow house across from the park in my hometown. One day in high school, I needed to borrow his car, and he was more than willing to let me use it. I backed it out of the garage and almost immediately heard a scraping sound. I'm sure I was saying, "No, no, no!" in my head as I jumped out and saw the damage. The chrome detailing on the right back fender was hanging straight out for all to see. I walked into the kitchen and found Grandpa at his usual seat at the kitchen table having a cookie. I told him the details of the accident and the damage to his car. He looked me straight in the eye and said, "Did you get hurt?" At that moment, I knew what forgiveness felt like. I knew what it was like to think about the other before thinking about yourself— and to put people over things. It was a time when compassion from Grandpa meant peace for me—and then we shared cookies.

Look at all these examples as a bountiful feast of choices, and then start choosing what you want. What are you hungry for at the age of sixty or seventy? Robert Louis Stevenson, a much more famous poet than me, wrote: "To know what you prefer, instead of humbly saying 'Amen' to what the world tells you ought to prefer, is to have kept your soul alive." [2]

One of my favorite books, possibly because I love the title so much, is *The Girls with the Grandmother Faces*, written in 1996 by Francis A. Weaver. She examines happiness and potential for those over fifty-five. [3] Step one is all about choices—"the long-lasting, ever-widening meaning of the choices we make." Her bottom-line advice is this: "One of the worst choices is not choosing at all." She reflects on this tendency for us to model our aging after our mothers and grandmothers. Of course, I want to make cookies for my grandchildren, but those cookies might not be available every day or even every month. Weaver puts it all on the table when she clearly states: "We cannot live like our grandmothers did, nor like our mothers. Women who don't maintain an active interest in the world around them are of no interest to anyone else. Failure to expand our own horizons is certain to lead to an old age of loneliness and boredom."

I recently enjoyed a lunch date with a few of my children, my husband, and my mother and father-in-law. We were at our favorite cafe, and it was time to order. I asked my mother-in-law what she was getting, and she said, "Well, the last time I was here, I noticed they had chicken salad and I told myself I would get that the next time I came ..." She paused before adding, "But Bob wants to split a hamburger, so I guess I'll do that." My mother-in-law is the most giving and unselfish person I know, so her response didn't surprise me, but it did make me take note. When I am eighty-six, married or not, I will order what I want to eat. From now on, I will call this my "Chicken Salad Aha Moment" and remember to concern myself with present things—that chicken salad was right there for the taking.

I can't write about my role models without mentioning Grandma Tommy. She was my husband's maternal grandmother and a fun-loving lady—the kind who would wear a Halloween mask to dinner at the assisted living when it wasn't even October. I recall visiting her one summer while she was spending time on Long Island with her daughter. It was a warm July day, and my husband and I decided to take her with us to Jones Beach. Her daughter was working, so we thought it would be a good way to spend the day. Having visited the beach as a child, Grandma Tommy was all in on the idea. That day, she sat in her chair with her toes in the sand and watched all the activity. It was a truly priceless afternoon with her. However, I still remember returning to her daughter's apartment later in the day and getting scolded by her daughter—because Grandma had gotten a bit sunburned. We were apologetic— but not regretful.

Go to the beach. Order the chicken salad. Bake the cookies. Play with your grandchildren.

To everything—turn, turn, turn—there is a season.

Your Turn

1. When you were a child, how old did you think your grandparents were? If you have children or grandchildren, ask them how old they think their grandparents are. Compare their perceptions to yours.

2. Who are your role models for aging now? Make a list of your top five. Have they changed over the past ten years? Identify one quality of your number-one role model that you would like to have and write it on a sticky note. Stick it somewhere you see every day, like your car dashboard or bathroom mirror, as a reminder to practice that quality daily.

3. Frances A. Weaver reminds us that "one of the worst choices is not choosing at all." Is there a situation currently in your life that you are "not choosing"? How might your day-to-day life change if you made a different choice or changed your perspective on your current situation?

Chapter Three

Culture

"Do not let your assumptions about a culture block your ability to perceive the individual, or you will fail."
Brandon Sanderson, *Words of Radiance*

We were a couple of days into our February road trip through New Zealand's South Island when we pulled our rental car into a scenic overlook. My husband and I, and two family members in their thirties, stood atop the Southern Alps admiring the view miles down into Queenstown. We all became fixated by one lone cyclist who was slowly and rhythmically climbing the steep grade toward the high point on the highway. The kind of mountain road that has a "check brakes" sign for those headed downhill. The cyclist's flame-orange vest brightly contrasted against the clay-red desert mountain. As the rider approached us at the peak, we applauded. We were expecting a thirty-something on their daily training ride up the peak. The rider rolled up to us and took off the helmet and visor to reveal an older woman with sun-worn skin. She introduced herself as Eleanor and proudly stated she was commemorating her seven decades of life with a bike trip across New Zealand. She had traveled from England and was thrilled to be experiencing each day in this stunning country. Her parting words to us before turning down the other side of the mountain were, "Make the most of every day because you don't get any back again."

Later at the coffee shop, sipping our flat whites, we all admitted our preconceived notions about who was riding that bike up that incredibly steep mountain. Our group comprised two physicians, a geriatric nurse, and a school guidance counselor—aging awareness/sensitivity, anyone? Anyone? No matter how much we have been trained or how much we value the older people in our lives, we still fall into those holes of ageism. We not only have preconceived notions about others' aging, but those of us turning sixty have those same low-bar notions about ourselves.

When will our cultural upbringing adjust to what aging really looks like in the twenty-first century? It might take a while, according to sociologist William F. Ogburn. Way back in 1922, he named this phenomenon *cultural lag.*[1] He described cultural lag as a tendency of material culture (technology, tools, things) to evolve and change rapidly, while non-material culture (values, morals, and religion) resists change and remains fixed for a far longer period of time. He predicted there would have to be a time of maladjustment as the non-material culture struggles to adapt to new material conditions. Indeed, just last night, I had a call from a friend who was frustrated at work because all the twenty-somethings in her office—who share her role—were completely ignoring her. She felt invisible. One even said, "Oh, this doesn't concern you." Another was shocked that my friend gave a perfectly relevant gift at the office Christmas gift exchange. "You picked this out?" she exclaimed. My friend is fifty-eight.

During my years working as a geriatric clinical nurse specialist, I had the pleasure of being a part of an interdisciplinary geriatric assessment team. Basically, we spent one full day a week evaluating an older adult whose family was seeking answers on living arrangements, memory loss, depression, medications, and declining function. One of the best questions I would ask the older adult client was, "How old would you be if you didn't know how old you were?" The answers were always quite telling. Those who considered themselves the most independent and happy often gave their age as ten, fifteen, sometimes twenty years younger than their chart indicated. I would hear things like, "Well, my knees feel like they are eighty, but the rest of me is maybe sixty." This type of response is supported by research from the Milken Institute and described in an intriguing book, *The Upside of Aging: How Long Life Is Changing the World of Health, Work, Innovation, Policy, and Purpose.* "Once people pass their fiftieth birthday, they tend to feel ten to fifteen years younger than their actual age," writes Ken Dychtwald about self-perception and aging. [2]

I fully believe in the saying that "age is just a number." However, when you have been told all your life that you can retire at age sixty-two, that you will need to go on Medicare at age sixty-five, and that you can get a discount on your pancakes at Perkins at age fifty-five—those numbers carry some clout. My girlfriends thought it was very funny to take me to Perkins to celebrate my fifty-fifth birthday. The next year we went back to the wine bar.

On August 10, 2019, social media guru Gary Vaynerchuk commented on people's inability to conceptualize time during an episode of his podcast, "Gary Vee." He said, "I know fifty- and sixty-year-olds who are wrapping it up. I tell them, 'Dude, you're only at half-time right now.'" [3]

This is our culture—we hear stories every day of friends and family who are "wrapping it up" in their late fifties or early sixties. The common questions I hear when I am in a group of sixty-somethings is, "When are you planning on retiring?" "Do you think you'd like to retire in Florida or Arizona?" "Are you more a beach person or a desert person?" Stories follow of family and friends who are navigating their seventies or eighties as snowbirds. Outwardly, I try to listen with rapt interest, but inside I'm feeling "meh." It seems that more than any other variable, the retirement years are associated with PLACE. If you are in your sixties (and Facebook knows it), your news-feed will be all about the best places to retire, as if choosing the right zip code will be the panacea for a meaningful third act.

I would love to have different stories to tell in my sixties and, hopefully, my seventies, eighties, and nineties. Stories that go beyond place and say more about purpose and people, significance and serendipity. I can change my story of aging, and you can change your story of aging, but if a whole bunch of us changed our stories, we could change the culture of aging.

Aging expert Ken Dychtwald suggests a different geometry. What if aging was cyclical rather than linear—a random movement of continual rebirths and reinventions in the areas of education, work, family, and leisure activities? Maybe I *can* still open that flower shop or sing in a bluegrass band—or both!

Peter Bregman, a thought leader in change management, believes that to change culture we need to do two simple things:

1. Do dramatic, story-worthy things that represent the culture we want to create.

2. Find other people who do story-worthy things that represent the culture we want to create. Then tell stories about them.[4]

Well, that sounds fun to me, how about you? As I turn sixty, I want to tell stories about myself and others that go beyond the stereotypical Medicare-card carrying, early-bird discount senior citizen. Don't get me wrong: Medicare has its place, and there's nothing wrong with going to dinner at 4:30 in the afternoon, but we all want to be more than that. Still, most of us have bought into the linear trajectory of life—learn, work, rest, die. That female cyclist I met in New Zealand was doing a story-worthy thing, and I am honored to share her story.

Marc Freedman in the *Upside of Aging* states that imagining new forms of aging will require innovation and creative thinking: "My suspicion is that none of this will happen without a social movement driven by those with the most to gain from the change, all of those over fifty who can enjoy a second chance at meaning and impact." [5]

There are lots of sixty-something storytellers around the world. According to a United Nations projection, in 2020, one billion people will be over sixty. This is a relatively new situation. The life expectancy in the early nineteen-hundreds was just forty-seven. [6] I recently attended the sixtieth birthday party of one of my closest girlfriends, Kirsten. It was an all-girl affair at our favorite wine bar, featuring lots of melted cheese, pesto, and potato chips. Perfection! The birthday girl has been by my side ever since we moved into the same dorm floor at college in the fall of 1977. Every month she would coach me through my unbearable menstrual cramps, and she even got me to ditch my 1970s-style eyeglasses for contact lenses. She has aged very well—likely due to her workout schedule and enviable ability to eat about 50 percent of what the rest of us usually do. There were many comments at the party that she doesn't look sixty, which she certainly does not. I also heard the phrase, "Sixty is the new forty." Well, realistically, and maybe happily, we are not living our forties over again. Our households look different, our job responsibilities have likely changed, and we are certainly a heck of a lot wiser. The storyline I want to write is this: "Sixty isn't the new forty; it's the new sixty!" [5] It's new because our culture hasn't adjusted to the health status and the possibilities we now have in our sixties, seventies, and eighties.

The possibilities—and the stories—are endless. I truly believe that narrative is currency, that each one of us is rich with stories that, when shared, can change our culture.

Your Turn

1. How old would you be if you didn't know how old you
    were? How would the world look if no one knew how old
    they were?

2. Consider Eleanor, the cyclist, at the beginning of this
    chapter. Would you travel alone? What would it look like?
    Write the destinations, the activities, and the food experi-
    ences you would choose.

3. What story could you tell today that would begin to change
    the culture of aging? It might be a story from your life or
    about someone you know who changes the stereotype of
    life after sixty. How could you share this story? Make it a
    goal to share this story with someone in your life this week.
    Learn from their response.

Chapter Four

Activity vs. Rest

> "Rest and self-care are so important. When you take time to replenish your spirit, it allows you to serve others from the overflow. You cannot serve from an empty vessel."
>
> **Eleanor Brown**

Everywhere you turn these days you can find information about how to slow down the aging process. Just stand in line at the grocery store and gaze to the left; you will find magazines touting miracle diets and easy five-minute workouts that you could probably be doing in the checkout line—c'mon multi-task! And you only need to consult your bathroom mirror or bathroom scale to be reminded that, yes, the physical changes of aging are real. Can we please order a new zippy metabolism from Amazon? Or how about a three-month supply of energy— and I don't mean a shipment of Red Bull. The complexity of aging of the human body was one of the main reasons I pursued a career in geriatric nursing in my twenties. All these years later, it is fascinating, and sometimes frightening, to be experiencing these changes in my own body. My first wakeup call was going through menopause in my fifties. I remember telling my doctor, "I feel thick and tired." It was the clearest way I could describe it.

It is not the purpose of this book to describe the changes that occur in our bodies as we accumulate birthdays. However, I will share some of the more common changes, especially those which I am personally experiencing and those that I feel, with some self-care mojo, can make the biggest impact on quality of life and, honestly, our ability to serve others: sleep, movement, water intake, and hearing. (Are you surprised by that last one? Stay tuned!) Turning my attention to these four areas of my physical health has resulted in two critical outcomes: strength and energy.

I am often inspired by watching my eighty-six-year-old mother-in-law make bread from scratch. She aggressively moves her arms, hands, and her fingers to knead every last bit of flour into a large, smooth dough ball. She tucks in the loose ends of dough until it fits perfectly into the familiar yellow glass bowl. One batch of homemade rolls in a day isn't enough. She moves on to *lefse*, a traditional thin Norwegian flatbread— emphasis on the thin. This is only accomplished by her rigorous rolling pin skills. The standing, bending, and muscular repetition of baking, and all kinds of housekeeping, give her strength for the journey—or, as my Grandma Marie would say in her gentle sighing voice, "It is better to wear out than to rust out."

As for energy, I will readily admit that completing menopause somewhere around age fifty-four was a magical boost to my overall wellbeing. The "thick and tired" feeling seemed to fade away (although the thick was probably still visible). I have worked to stay in a rhythm of self-care, and some days I am more successful than others. Forgiving oneself is the most powerful form of self-care, and I do it abundantly. However, the days when I exercise, make healthy food choices, stay mobile, and engage in meaningful social interactions and service are the days I feel the best. The extrovert in me is instantly energized by the prospect of hosting guests for dinner or an invitation to coffee with a friend. I know what works for me, and I'm sure that, deep down, you know what works for you. A book and a cup of tea may be more your style, but I would encourage you to test out those patterns and rhythms that result in strength and energy *for you*. Journaling can be a valuable tool for later examination and reflection.

Remember, narrative is currency. Your own daily story jotted in a notebook or journal can later be priceless information for yourself or your healthcare provider.

Let's dive into my favorite self-care activity. I love to sleep. I believe sleep is the most natural method of healing and the perfect example of self-care. I remember in my thirties and forties, I would often stay up until midnight or 1:00 AM doing office work, or maybe writing a grant, or working on a volunteer project for the school PTA. I look back at those years in disbelief because I know I couldn't (or wouldn't) do that now (maybe that is the definition of wisdom). Comedian Mindy Kaling captures my love of sleep when she writes: "There is no sunrise so beautiful that it is worth waking me up to see it."[1]

One of my favorite lectures I gave as a geriatric clinical nurse specialist was on sleep. I would describe the changes that occur with aging and the habits of good "sleep hygiene" to practice prior to bedtime, such as taking a hot bath or going for a walk at least two hours before you want to fall asleep. I would often ask the audience if they were "night owls" or "dawn larks." It is typical that most of us become larks as we age, but even today, I still don't want to be woken for the sunrise. I would also ask my audience, "Do you feel rested and refreshed in the morning?" They may have woken a couple of times for a trip or two to the bathroom, but if they awoke in the morning and felt rested, that is considered a good night's sleep.

Our sleep patterns do become more erratic as we age, and we have to stay in bed longer to get our needed seven or eight hours of sleep. My twenty-one-year-old son, Mason, can hit the pillow and be sound asleep within minutes and not wake up until his alarm goes off in the morning. His so-called "sleep efficiency" is 100 percent. I, on the other hand, am probably awake one or two hours of the nine hours I am in bed, so my sleep efficiency is around 75 percent.

It is valuable to be aware of patterns in all parts of your life, especially in your sleep. Keep some notes and look for what factors seem to make you have a good night or bad night. I, sadly, lose significant sleep efficiency whenever I have a rich chocolate dessert following dinner. I think it's time to start having my cake for breakfast.

We are, to a great extent, the architects of our own sleep. A friend of mine just discovered the use of meditation to greatly improve her sleep. My personal trick is to take five deep, long breaths in and out whenever I find myself awake at night. Clear out that old carbon dioxide and breathe in some fresh oxygen.

Moving on to the matter of movement. If you've been sitting and reading awhile, it's time to turn your head, change positions, do some stretches, or stand up and walk a bit. My nursing language would state I need to balance activity vs. rest. It's rare that I'm tipping the scales towards too much activity, since it's so easy to do the resting part—especially if you add in the desk and couch time. It is now recommended that those sitting at desk jobs for eight hours a day need to move around forty times a day, and we should only be sitting for thirty minutes at a time. In this lifestyle of scrolling on phones and binge-watching TV shows, I'm the first to raise my hand and say, "That's me!"

Apparently, sitting is so unhealthy that it is the new smoking. Let's all say it together: "Sitting is the new smoking!" Humans are meant to be upright and active, and sitting for prolonged periods of time impacts the effectiveness of your heart and cardiovascular system, the alignment of your spine, and even your bowel function. A Canadian study followed 17,000 citizens aged seventeen to ninety for twelve years to measure the connection between sitting time and mortality. It found that the number of hours per day spent sitting was associated with an elevated risk of death from all causes, except cancer. Additionally, the risks from sitting were not mitigated by occasional leisure-time physical activity.[2]

My yoga instructor, Gretchen, helped me clearly understand the impact of sitting during a recent class. She used a vivid image of our hips after too much sitting: "Our hips are the 'root' of our body. It's where the first and second chakra are located, and everything pushes down to that root. Unfortunately, our hips also become our junk drawer. Our goal is to keep the tightness cleared out and the energy stabilized." She went on to share this illustration: "I like to picture it this way. When you pour salt into a glass of water, it falls to the bottom of the glass. That doesn't have much purpose, does it? We need it dispersed throughout the whole glass of water. It won't dissolve until you add some heat or some movement. So, picture yourself stirring up that salt!" She says this while rotating her torso as if it were a spoon in a glass.

This lesson would have been a valuable image to use when I was working on a fall prevention project with senior citizens in the community during my geriatric nursing practice. I would teach them a series of easy kitchen-sink exercises, which if completed twice a day over a period of three months would decrease falls by one-third, according to the nurse researchers. I should probably start doing these myself:

Stand at the kitchen sink with your hands resting on the counter for support.

First, stand on tiptoes and feel the stretch in your legs for at least five seconds.

Lower your heels to the floor and stand flat on your feet. Repeat five times.

Second, lift one leg and stand balanced for five to fifteen seconds.

Switch legs. Repeat five times.

A simple kitchen exercise that will really clear out your "junk drawer" requires your best hula-hoop moves: Rotate your pelvis to the right and then to the left five times each way. An easy routine to add to your day!

My clients found these exercises helpful because they had noticed the loss of flexibility in their hips, and the exercises seemed approachable and safe. Any of us, at any age, can trip on a toy in the living room or miss the last step of our stairway, but improving one's lower-leg strength, balance, and flexibility makes one less prone to falling.

If you're looking for ways to avoid sitting too long, here are a few tips that you may find easy and fun to build into your daily routine:

- Go fill your dog's bowl.
- Park your phone somewhere.
- Use your kitchen counter as a standing desk.
- Play vinyl records instead of streaming. They only last fifteen minutes per side, and so you'll need to get up to flip to side B. Add some dance moves before sitting back down!
- Walk during phone calls. Bonus vitamin D points if you do this outdoors on a sunny day.

- Plan standing or walking meetings instead of sitting at the coffee shop.

I'm not an athlete. I play a bit of tennis, but I truly don't enjoy exercising. I have committed to doing yoga and Pilates each week, and I try to walk every day, but I'm not proud to say that I do the minimal daily requirement in the exercise department. My husband loves to do projects around the house and yard, and I'm often called on to carry a piece of furniture or steady a telephone pole while he builds a suspension bridge (not exaggerating here!). I credit my balance, strength, and body awareness to yoga and Pilates. And they have helped me avoid injuries. I'll happily go with my kids skiing once or twice a year; and the goal is always to not fall or get hurt. So far, I've met that goal each time.

Even if exercise isn't your passion, committing to some form of activity, however minimal, will reap rewards in so many areas of your life. Start small and see where it turns. When I gather with friends and we talk about health, it's usually not about the lab values from our online medical record or the number of pounds we have gained since our last birthday. The conversation usually focuses on activities—carrying grandchildren or carrying groceries, playing tennis, shoveling snow, or standing on a ladder to clean the gutters—and let's not forget the challenge of opening a pickle jar (grip strength is a measurement of aging). It's not physical health we're talking about; it's functional health. Is your [insert age]-year-old body able to do what you need to do to live the life you want to live?

Assessing functional health was my favorite part of my

geriatric nursing practice. Basically, I was trying to determine if the body was doing everything the client needed it to do to complete activities that were important to him or her. One woman was very clear in what she needed from her body: "I want to be able to kneel at Mass." But her knees would not allow that, so a physical therapy consultation was ordered. Others had a goal to continue to drive their car to the post office—call in the occupational therapist. Others want to be able to carry their grandchildren free of back pain or do their own laundry. At sixty, I can say my goal is to still be able to ski with my kids. What are your functional health desires?

When I worked in the faith community nursing setting, we often discussed the concept of being "fit to serve." Being able to volunteer in the community or serve as a caregiver was often a motivator to add exercise to one's daily routine. My older sister is the proud grandma of eight granddaughters under the age of eight. What are the odds? After Granddaughter Number Two, some hip, back, and neck pain from typical childcare activities made her realize that she needed to do something. She committed to a routine of yoga and Pilates and is now ready to carry, console, and cuddle as much as needed—pain free.

My dad often said, "It's tough to get old." The phrase was usually associated with some kind of necessary movement. I can picture him in the cornfield trying to climb into the big green combine during harvest or exiting his La-Z-Boy chair after a post-lunch nap. I now catch myself saying, "Yes, Dad, it's tough to get old." But can my generation have a more positive mantra about aging and movement than my dad's? The research suggests we can.

A recent collaborative study completed at the University of Birmingham in Alabama and King's College in London compared two groups of people, both men and women, ages fifty-five to eighty. One group were active cyclists who were able to bike more than thirty-five miles in six hours. The comparison group did not take part in regular exercise. Neither group included smokers, heavy drinkers, or those with high blood pressure. The study found that no loss of muscle mass and strength existed in the active exercise group, and their body fat and cholesterol levels had not increased related to their age. Most surprisingly, though, was that their immune systems matched those of a much younger person. One of the researchers, Dr. Niharika Arora Duggal, said: "We hope these findings prevent the danger that, as a society, we accept that old age and disease are normal bedfellows and that the third age of man is something to be endured and not enjoyed."[3] Sorry, Dad, your mantra is being debunked, and that gets me excited.

From my previous exercise confession, you'll know I am clearly not biking thirty-odd miles a day. I'm not sure they make bike shorts padded enough to make that pleasant for me. However, I do like to walk the country roads near our home and check on the neighbor's horses. The most recent guidelines from Health and Human Services recommends 150 minutes per week of moderate-intensity aerobic activity spread throughout the week; for example, a walk at a speed of two and a half miles per hour or biking less than ten miles per hour. Even raking the yard fits their prescription. New to these guidelines is the importance of muscle strengthening activity two days a week. Use resistance bands or hand weights to work a variety of muscle groups. You may want to pump those grocery bags before you empty them![4]

How about my twice-weekly Pilates? Consider this title on a Pilates website that quickly caught my eye: "How Pilates Makes You Ageless." It goes into a discussion of posture and its impact on appearance: "The pain and discomfort caused by poor posture is a factor in making people appear older. Look around you and see how being stooped and rounded detracts from one's appearance. A seventy-year-old who stands tall and erect with a graceful gait can look as much as fifteen years younger."[5] So, let's *turn* our shoulders back and *turn* our gaze forward. Just as we used to hear that "stand up straight" command from our mothers, let's whisper it in our own ears today.

Your Turn

1. What are your functional health goals? Is your body capable of doing everything you need it to do today? If not, what would you like it to be better at? Write down a list of three functional health goals you'd like to accomplish in the next year.

2. Is there a new activity you would like to try? What would it be, and what benefits can you imagine might occur from doing it? Write down five new activities and choose one to try this week. Send a photo of your new adventure to a friend or family member.

3. What strategies help you sleep better? What commitment would you like to make to yourself to assure better sleep? Make a note of this and put it on your bedside table or as a phone reminder each evening.

Chapter Five

The Power of a Scoop of Water

"For I was hungry and you gave me something to eat, I was thirsty and you gave me something to drink, I was a stranger and you invited me in."

Matthew 25:35

There was one Saturday evening each year during my childhood that was always more exciting than any of the others. It was the one Saturday evening that *Cinderella* was broadcast on national television. You probably have your own preferred version of *Cinderella*, but the Rodgers & Hammerstein theatrical version with the simple pastel set and almost no special effects will always be my favorite. Oh, how I loved pretending to be Lesley Ann Warren singing, "In my own little corner, in my own little chair, I can be whatever I want to be." I can still recall nearly every scene. The climax of the movie came when the prince went searching for Cinderella the day after the magical ball where she lost her glass slipper. Her wise fairy godmother facilitated the reunion by telling Cinderella to go outside and offer the prince—who was just about to leave—a dip of cool water from the well. Cinderella quickly goes outside and bravely speaks to the prince: "You have traveled far. You are sad, weary, and thirsty." He gladly accepts the scoop of water and within seconds recognizes her—and they lived happily ever after.[1]

On a more recent Saturday, a scoop of water was used to remember my daughter's baptism. It was on her wedding day in 2019, and she and her soon-to-be husband stood by the baptismal font in our church as our pastor scooped up water and spoke these words: "Julia and Luke, dearly beloved of God, when you make your promises to one another, you will draw from the deep well of the promises God made to you the day you were baptized in Christ: to make a home with you wherever you live, to clothe you with forgiveness and mercy, to send you as light into the world, and to give you abundant life in Jesus Christ."[2] They turned to each other and declared their intention to bind themselves together in the covenant of marriage.

The power of a scoop of water is that it can refresh our parched souls, serve a thirsty love, and remind us of promises. It is truly life giving, but we certainly take it for granted and might even describe it as ordinary. It may be this ordinariness that causes us to often forget about the healing power that water brings to our thirsty bodies, minds, and souls.

I have often heard the adage that if you feel thirsty, you are already dehydrated, so I am trying to change my behavior in this area. I recently purchased a water bottle that has positive messages written on it, such as "Do it for yourself," "Keep going," and "Tons of energy." When I ordered it, I wasn't aware it would be so large that I had to stand at the kitchen counter to drink from it. This thing holds a gallon of water! I drove around in my car with it buckled into the passenger seat! I've only had it for about ten days, but I do feel more awake and am avoiding that 4:00 p.m. sleepy time when all I want is a nap or a cookie, or both.

There are all kinds of reasons to drink more water. I love this list from *Medical News Today*: [3]

- It lubricates the joints.
- It forms saliva and mucus.
- It delivers oxygen throughout the body (our blood is 90 percent water).
- It boosts skin health and beauty.
- It cushions the brain, spinal cord, and other sensitive tissues.
- Prolonged dehydration can impact thinking and reasoning.
- It regulates body temperature.
- The digestive system depends on it.
- It flushes body waste.
- It helps maintain blood pressure.

- The airways need it.
- It makes minerals and nutrients accessible.
- It prevents kidney damage.
- It boosts performance during exercise.
- It helps with weight loss, if it is consumed instead of caloric drinks (like juices or sodas).

Okay, let's discuss the elephant in the room here. Yes, you will need to go to the bathroom more often—possibly much more often. I've certainly noticed that. In fact, I feel like I'm back to the days when my kids were little, when I knew the location of every decent bathroom in our town. Once again, it is wise to strategically plan to use the bathroom at least every two hours. Bottom line: by drinking water generously throughout your day, you are allowing it to do what it is meant to do.

Offering a scoop of water to others is an act of kindness. Who of us can walk by a wilting flower or herb without wanting to give it a drink? When I was practicing nursing in the hospital, the first thing I would do whenever I entered a patient's room was to offer them a glass of water. Usually, my practice involved lots of interview questions, and the water gesture primed the pump, so to speak. How can you add this routine to your daily interactions with friends and family? Tip: Use your prettiest glasses to make drinking water a more pleasurable experience!

In what other ways do you use water for self-care? Do you love to jump into a clear, cold lake on a hot summer day? Hike to a nearby waterfall? Maybe soaking in a hot tub is more your style. In whatever way you encounter this daily gift, be sure to add a response of thanks to God the Creator who gave it to us. Isak Dinesen, a Danish writer, whose moving memoir, *Out of Africa*, inspired the classic movie by the same name, wrote her view of the healing power of water. "I know of a cure for everything: salt water ... sweat, or tears or the salt sea."[4] (Isak Dinesen is the pen name of Karen Christence Dinesen, who lived from 1885 to 1962, for many of those years in her beloved Africa. She wrote into her sixties, and her fiction and nonfiction titles are drinks for a thirsty soul.)

I know the ocean is a saltwater cure for this Midwest girl. I recall sitting on a beach in Florida and being mesmerized by the scampering sandpipers. Probably no bigger than six inches long, the birds flocked along the shoreline, very near the water's edge, to quickly feed on whatever crustacean treat the next wave would uncover. They were so careful not to get caught up in the wave; as soon as it came towards them, they turned and darted inland. As I watched them, I felt that I was one of those sandpipers and the waves were the waters of my baptism. Most days, I don't let myself be drenched by the water and promises made to me at my baptism—and the ones remembered at Julia and Luke's wedding. Rather, I turn the other way, like a scampering sandpiper and follow my own voice rather than these words spoken at the Sacrament of Holy Baptism: "In Holy Baptism, God liberates us from sin and death by joining us to the death and resurrection of our Lord Jesus Christ. Born children of a fallen humanity, in the baptismal waters, we become God's reborn children and inherit eternal life. By water and the Holy Spirit, we are made members of the Church, which is Christ's body. As we live with him and with his people, we grow in faith, love, and obedience to God's will." [5]

That scoop of water put on my head when I was a baby in 1959 still drenches me today. It "endures" as my friend, author and theologian Ken Jones says. Baptism is present tense; I *am* baptized. [6] Just as Cinderella became royalty through a scoop of water, so did I. I inherited God's kingdom on my baptism day.

Let's enjoy more scoops of water and live like the princes and princesses we are!

Your Turn

1. Close your eyes and picture your favorite body of water.
    What does it look like? Where is it? How does it make you
    feel? If it is a positive experience, tuck it in your memory
    to use as a relaxation exercise.

2. If you have been baptized, has your knowledge of baptism
    changed throughout your life? Read Matthew 3: 13-17
    about Jesus' baptism. Try to write a six-word story about
    your own baptism. This could become a simple mantra to
    begin each new day. My six-word story: God's promises
    pour over me today.

3. If you had the chance to give a cool and energizing glass of
    water to anyone, who would you want to give it to? What
    words would you say?

Chapter Six

Do You Hear What I Hear?

"The world is full of magic things, patiently waiting for
our senses to grow sharper."

W.B. Yeats

I believe we are all here to live an abundant life, which includes
the experiences that our senses make vivid—sight, smell, taste,
hearing, and touch. Life is beautiful through the prism of each
of these miracles. My vision is 20/400 without my glasses or con-
tacts, and it has been that way since childhood. Getting my first
pair of glasses in fifth grade rocked my world and put leaves on
the trees. The fact that I would have been considered legally blind
in another century is not lost on me. I am thankful for the vision
technology of our times, and that includes progressive lenses.

Take a deep breath in. What do you smell? As I write, my nose is sensing a wet dog—I hope you're connecting with something more fragrant! Your sense of smell may decrease as you age, especially if you have chronic sinus problems. Did you know that your sense of smell can invoke a memory faster than seeing an old photograph or hearing a favorite song? For example, when I smell popcorn, I am immediately transported to Grandma Johnson's kitchen, where she made popcorn in an electric skillet on her kitchen table—shake, shake, shake. The same table where I told Grandpa I "crashed" his car. And today, as I rode my bike through my neighborhood, I caught a whiff of my neighbor's pine trees heavy with morning dew. I live in the relatively flat "east river" part of South Dakota, but suddenly I was 400 miles away, among the pine trees at Outlaw Ranch Bible Camp in the Black Hills, back in 1978. I was leading a bunch of seventh-grade girls from our A-frame cabin to breakfast at the mess hall. My sense of smell turned back time. Tune in to the power of this sense and see where it takes you.

The magical delight of taste really goes without saying, right friends? The number of taste buds decrease as we age and the ones that remain tend to lose some of their sensitivity. Smoking, certain illnesses, and some medications can also impact our ability to taste. You may have noticed you need more seasoning now than when you were younger, or you might be gravitating towards spicier foods. Now is the time to keep turning to new foods that you may have not yet experienced or ones you thought you wouldn't like. Seeing and tasting God's abundant creation of spices and herbs, fruits and vegetables could be a fun focus if you're bored with your current meal situation. Exposing our taste buds to a variety of flavors can keep our sense of taste more vital as we age. So, it might be time to organize a cooking club or lunch-bunch group to try new recipes or new restaurants.

One of the great joys of my life has been our co-ownership of two beautiful wineries—Jessup Cellars and Handwritten Wines—located in the quaint village of Yountville, in the Napa Valley of California. We have discovered learning opportunities and surprises with each visit we make. Wine tasting is a great way to hone one's sense of smell and taste. It's a beneficial and beautiful exercise that translates into a more acute awareness of all food and drink. There is also a slowness to the entire wine tasting process that allows all your senses to participate at a high level—a wonderful way to feed your soul and your memory bank.

As much as I love to taste and smell and touch and see, the sense that I treasure is the one that has been most impacted by my aging: my hearing. However, in the last few years, I've become more acutely aware of the sounds around me—background music, conversations in the checkout line, and my daughter's voice across the kitchen table. You see, I did a thing about four years ago. I got hearing aids. That name didn't resonate with me, so I call them my "ear candy" because they make day-to-day life sweeter for me and those around me.

Prior to these two little computers in my ears, I was constantly saying, "Excuse me?" "Could you repeat that?" "What did you say?" I got good at smiling and nodding in fake understanding; worse yet, sometimes I just tuned out. Full disclosure: I still do these things depending on the setting, but I have to pretend or check out much less often now.

What else did I notice? Prior to receiving my ear candy, I was frequently exhausted from listening intently and then doing the mental gymnastics necessary to determine what I think the person most likely said. I'm sure my family and friends can recall many times when my mental gymnastics failed and I simply did not hear.

So, how do you get someone to visit their local audiologist? Let me share what my creative husband did. He informed me that he made appointments "for both of us" because he was concerned about *his* hearing and thought I might as well get checked, too. Sneaky. He also shared some medical wisdom that grabbed my attention. He said it is better to get hearing aids sooner rather than later. Apparently, if you wait too long, your brain can forget how to hear and won't respond as well to the amplification.[1] Our date with the audiologist was painless and predictable—I needed hearing correction, my husband didn't.

The process of getting fitted for my ear candy was fascinating. Both the expertise of my audiologist and the technology available were amazing. It was one of those times in my life when I am glad I live in the twenty-first century. (Side note: I also got to choose a color for those bad boys; not unlike choosing paint color for a new car.) I remember clearly the day I received my ear candy. My daughter and I were in the elevator leaving the clinic, and she still laughs thinking how I jumped when I heard the elevator DING. The things I must have been missing! I got in the car and had to turn the volume down on my radio about 50 percent. She and I had a great conversation on the way home without a single "What?"

I admit I avoided wearing my hair in a ponytail for several months after getting my ear candy. I've since come to my senses on that (honestly, these things are so small that they're barely noticeable), and now my goal is to make wearing ear candy cool. I might even go back to my fifth-grade pixie haircut. Stay tuned on that.

My goals for my self-care actions are always twofold: strength and energy. I asked an audiologist friend, Noreen, about the energy I have felt the last couple of years since getting my hearing aids. She told me, "There is a huge fatigue factor with hearing loss. The listening effort that you have to expend each day takes away energy from other tasks." Scientifically, the listening effort is referred to as Cognitive Load Theory, and it provides a reasonable explanation for why hearing aids enhance listeners' working memory and executive function. [2] When listeners spend less effort on the primary task of understanding speech, they have more capacity to remember key information, eliminate unnecessary information, and perform the secondary task quickly. [1] In fact, many researchers are now curious to find out if offering more hearing evaluation and treatments would decrease the number of older adults who experience cognitive decline. A fascinating and hopeful field of inquiry.

Noreen suggested a common-sense approach to hearing loss: "Just as weight creeps up on us as we age, or sun exposure accumulates, or gum disease increases, hearing loss creeps up on us, too. It is so much easier to deal with it early on." So, if you're watching your calories, visiting your dermatologist, or going to your dentist regularly, you might as well add an audiology appointment to your calendar.

Noreen also shared a fascinating observation regarding the social stigma of wearing hearing aids, which I understood after my initial refusal to show them off. People wearing them used to be perceived as being old or impaired. Happily, she says the stigma has almost disappeared. The reason? So many people wear some kind of in-ear device, be it wireless earbuds or Bluetooth headsets that ear candy seems to go unnoticed. She adds, "Interestingly, the stigma is gone in the general public, but it's still common among those who wear hearing aids." Not me, not anymore. How about you? It might be time to make a date with your friend or spouse and head to the local audiologist.

For those of you fortunate enough to not be experiencing hearing loss, here's a self-care idea for you: Resolve to protect the hearing capabilities that you currently have. Wear hearing protection (earplugs) at concerts or other loud environments, when operating machinery, or hunting, and be smart when listening to podcasts and music through headphones. Keep those inexpensive foam earplugs handy and hand them out like candy.

Your Turn

1. Do you have a favorite sense? How does it bring you abundant life?

2. Have you ever been fatigued from one of your senses not functioning well? How did it impact your daily activities?

3. Make a sensory to-do list for your day. List each of the five senses and write down one thing you want to do today to experience and awaken your senses of hearing, sight, touch, taste, and smell. Next, write down one thing you can do today to protect each of those senses.

Chapter Seven

Ears Open and Head Up

"He strode down the street with his mouth full of
harmony and his soul full of gratitude."
Mark Twain, *The Adventures of Tom Sawyer*

The list of things I have learned from being a part of the Blue
family for nearly forty years is quite long. I will be forever
grateful to my mother-in-law for teaching me how to bake a
stellar pie crust and to my father-in-law for his bold compli-
ments. I recall staying at their home for the first time when
my husband, Dan, and I were dating. Over the course of the
weekend my father-in-law stated that "I had a lot of hair"—
thank you 1970s—and "I was a good eater." I wasn't sure if he
thought his son had brought home a girlfriend or a horse.

The most practical thing I have learned from them is their family whistle—a quick *whi-whi-whi-whi-whi*. It is pure magic. Any of us in the bloodline—our children included—are trained to hear this whistle and will perk up like a pointer puppy when hearing it. It has been immensely helpful on family trips to Disneyland, on a remote hiking trail, or simply in line at McDonald's.

Our family whistle is unique and helps me stay connected with my family. But I have another more powerful connection that I hear daily, when I take time to listen. My faith tradition as a Christian has given me a different, more powerful voice—that is the voice of Christ as proclaimed in John 10:27: "My sheep hear my voice, and I know them, and they follow me."

How does God do that? How does God promise that we—his sheep—hear his voice? I imagine the big Mickey ears our kids would wear in Disneyland—the black felt hats that had their names stylishly stitched on the back. Mickey must have great hearing; I'm envious. So, where do I get some big ears—besides Disneyland? As a Christian, I received the Holy Spirit and became a child of God at the time of my baptism. The mystery of having the Holy Spirit actually inside me has taken me years to understand, even though I've stood at the baptismal font for my own children and for my godchildren. I now realize that it is not for me to fully understand, but rather to fully believe. I have come to this conclusion: the Holy Spirit is not my cheerleader (though I could really use one); rather, the Holy Spirit works in a different way. The Holy Spirit sends me a preacher; the preacher brings me the Gospel; the Gospel is the good news of Christ's forgiveness. When I am a forgiven child of God, I am free to turn my ear to hear the voice of my neighbor. The Holy Spirit gives me *big ears*. I have to admit, I always trust the sound of the Blue family whistle, but do I always trust the sound of the Gospel? Unfortunately, no.

It's a daily struggle to tune into God's Word. I could certainly help the process by opening my Bible, but I don't always do that. Daily prayer is usually part of my routine, but sometimes the background noise of my own voice drowns out my intentions. That tricky devil gets in my ear and it sounds just like my voice: "I look like I'm eighty," or "No one cares what I'm doing," or "Why did we invite company over tonight? My house is a mess!" or "I'm so scared that I will be left alone."

My daily challenge is to hear Christ's voice and not my own. I have heard a preacher say that we are on a cycle of daily dying and rising. We are released from our burdens each day, but we try to take them back. Why? Because we fall in love with our "prison," our "rut." It feels safe and familiar. The good news is that God will not give up on you. He will put these words in your ear: "I forgive you. You are free!"

When my kids and my husband hear our family whistle, they perk up, set their gaze on the whistler, and turn to whatever activity is next or to whomever needs their help. What would life be like if I were tuned into that whistle all day? I couldn't stop myself from doing a dance called "Turn, turn, turn." I'd be like the sheep in the scripture above, which says, "My sheep hear my voice ... and they follow me." With no to-do list or goals to accomplish for the day, the week, or the year; I would simply listen for the whistle and turn, turn, turn. Let's substitute God's forgiveness for the Blue family whistle. How would you feel if whatever burdens or worries or sins you are carrying were lifted from you with the simple Gospel words of "I forgive you; you are free"?

In the first chapter, when I broached the topic of a personal faith, I listed some things our hearts might be pinned to rather than Jesus—including, our families, job, food, shopping, or an unending grief. I said we have a natural tendency to weigh all these things on our birthdays. As you reach your next birthday, your family might not be bringing you joy, your job may be coming to an end, or an addiction may be your daily prison. All these things and more can weigh you down. The Good Shepherd can whisper in your ear, "You are enough" and release you from that weight. It's like the flight attendant announcing that you are "free to move about the cabin."

I am here to tell you that, if you live by faith and the trust that Christ brings you each day, you'll be doing far more interesting and exciting things than just walking down the aisle of an airplane. What does "living by faith" look like? Lutheran scholar Steve Paulson uses this analogy: "Faith looks like a drop of water clinging to a cool pitcher on a hot summer day. You are clinging to the voice of the shepherd." Just imagine that. [1]

You may have noticed I've taken a 180-degree turn since the previous chapter on self-care and am asking you to not think so much about yourself. I did a fair amount of my own navel gazing telling you about my exercise routine, my sleep, and my lack of fluid intake. Sorry. Isn't that just typical? One of my pet peeves is calling a friend or family member and before I can even say how my day is going, I've learned everything about their latest pain, party, or purchase. But this is human nature. This is self-interest. This is what Luther calls *incurvatus in se*—that's Latin for "navel gazing." Luther writes: "Scripture describes man as so curved in upon himself that he uses not only physical but even spiritual goods for his own purposes and in all things seeks only himself." [2]

I try to turn my gaze towards others, but it is human nature to look at oneself. We are often unconscious of this fact, even as it drives our behavior. Can we learn to live outside of ourselves? Can we avoid becoming our own project? Even this book appears to be a project about turning sixty. Rather than conforming to the ways of aging in the world, should we not be transforming ourselves on behalf of the world?

Remember when I said that good posture can make you look fifteen years younger? What if we take that physical improvement in posture that increases lung capacity and decreases pain and add the habit of turning to our neighbor described above? In the words of J.J. on the 1970s sitcom *Good Times*—that would be "DY-NO-MITE!" We crave wholeness as we age, a wholeness of body, mind, and spirit. Having big ears for the gospel of forgiveness and then turning to hear the call of your neighbor are the one-two punch the doctor ordered.

Let us not be weighed down by a plan, a purpose, or priorities, but rather assume a posture that is open to what the world needs.

Your Turn

1. Take fifteen minutes in your home, workplace, or a favorite spot outdoors and try writing down or noting the sounds you hear. What sorts of sounds are most common? How does being surrounded by these sounds affect your daily life and routine?

2. Have you been hearing a "calling" from a neighbor, family member, or your community, near or far? Are you moved to answer that call? What might be the risks and rewards from doing so?

3. Whose voice do you most often hear in your head? Is it your own? Words from others? God's words of promise or forgiveness? Write down the words you would like to hear.

Chapter Eight

The Wonder Years

"He who can no longer pause to wonder and stand rapt
in awe is as good as dead; his eyes are closed."
Albert Einstein

One of my favorite words is "wonder." It not only captures so
much about what I value in life, it is also a lovely word to say.
Wonder. For fellow language lovers, let's ponder the breadth
of that word. It's a noun, a verb, an adjective, and the last name
of one of my favorite musical artists. (I really hope someone
sings "Isn't She Lovely?" to me on my ninetieth birthday). I
like the *Oxford English Dictionary's* definition best: "A feeling
of amazement and admiration, caused by something beautiful,
remarkable, or unfamiliar." Sigh. Isn't that just lovely?

At the reading of this chapter's title, you may have already time traveled back to the era of the TV classic *The Wonder Years*. It was a popular television show in the late 1980s, and the storyline recalled the junior high and high school years of Kevin, Winnie, and friends from 1968 to 1973. The static-filled home movie intro is filled with the characters, the clothes, and the cars of 1968—it's our childhood all over again. Fittingly, the background music of the first episode is "Turn, Turn, Turn," sung by The Byrds, and the narrator comments, "Those really were the wonder years for us there in the suburbs and kind of a 'golden age' for kids." [1] I know I feel this way about my childhood, and maybe you feel the same about yours.

In 2019, Kevin and Winnie turned sixty, along with many of us. Could we reprise our wonder years? Could we, as the dictionary describes, find amazement and admiration caused by something beautiful, remarkable, or unfamiliar? I believe we can if we allow our heads and ears and eyes and hearts to be turned in new directions. Maybe the direction won't even be new, but maybe we'll see a friend in a new light or hear their voice in a clearer tone. I'm looking forward to finding people, experiences, and locations that ignite wonder in me.

I made a new friend a couple of weeks ago. She was a part of a group wine tasting at our Handwritten tasting room in Yountville. Her gracious spirit and curiosity caught my attention as we spent nearly three hours around a table learning from our knowledgeable and charming wine educator, Bill, about our wines. I was intrigued by her history, which included a college degree in home economics and a business career in home designs, but mostly I was interested in the fact she had completed a thirty-four-page research paper on fudge. This sixty-something girl knew her fudge! It was, in fact, fascinating, and she was happy to share her expertise. The other thing I admired was that she knew how to ask questions without any fear of looking silly.

As she listened intently to Bill and followed his instructions on how to distinguish scents and flavors in the wine, I could see a sense of wonder on her face. After the tasting was done, she said to me, "This has been one of the best things I have ever done in my life." Her eyes were wide open, and her voice was sincere and grateful. Her admiration was evident. Experiences such as this are what make a good life into a great life. Beautiful, remarkable, and unfamiliar experiences can be found outside the front door, inside a book, or on a subway. You only need to turn.

In 2002, when my father-in-law was turning seventy, I stopped at the bookstore on the way to his house to pick up a birthday gift. I wandered around looking for something that might be inspiring to him. The cover of a coffee-table book that featured a vintage Chris-Craft wooden boat caught my eye. I recall that my father-in-law had built his own small wooden boat when he was a teenager and loved recounting stories about that adventure. This history book featuring plenty of photos would be perfect. As a geriatric nurse, I love gifts that provoke reminiscing. Well, as it turned out, this gift went way beyond reminiscing. Not only did my father-in-law pore over every word and picture he also became inspired to build a full-size replica of a 1942 Triple Cockpit Chris-Craft wooden boat. This wasn't a kit; he tracked down plans and spent three summers in his woodshop completing this handmade beauty that is 23 feet long, 8 feet wide and 5 feet tall. When asked recently if he ever questioned beginning such a big project, he responded, "Never. I enjoyed those three summers as much or more than any summers I've had." He finished it at age seventy-four. One of our fondest family memories is being with him in that boat for its maiden voyage. It worked like a charm, except for the fact that when you turned the steering wheel to the left, the boat went to the right. That was fixed in time for the next ride. He named the boat *Chicky*—his pet name for my mother-in-law. The golden script letters of *Chicky* grace the back of this stately and sleek mahogany boat as it now rests in grandpa's garage. He still uncovers it occasionally, along with lots of stories, for curious visitors who look and listen in wonder.

Do you believe that you could have your best summers ahead of you? If not, how do we put more wonder into our lives? One of my favorite Christmas hymns is "I Wonder as I Wander."[2] I have an affinity for haunting minor-key melodies and alliteration. The words are printed here, and there are many beautiful renditions on YouTube.

> I wonder as I wander out under the sky,
> How Jesus the Savior did come for to die
> For poor on'ry people like you and like I.
> I wonder as I wander out under the sky.
> When Mary birthed Jesus 'twas in a cow's stall

With wise men and farmers and shepherds and
all,
But high from God's heaven a star's light did fall.
And the promise of ages it then did recall.
If Jesus had wanted for any wee thing
A star in the sky, or a bird on the wing
Or all of God's angels in heav'n for to sing
He surely could have it, 'cause he was the King!

If you wander out under the sky, chances are you are turning your head to look around, up, down, and outside of yourself. You're using all your senses to notice the brightest stars, the tiniest blooms, the sounds of cicadas, and even a neighbor in need—things that are often obscured by our own voice in our heads or our own lack of vision outside of ourselves.

I am taken by the hymn's use of the word "on'ry." John Jacob Niles published the song in 1934, after hearing it sung by a young traveling preacher, Annie Morgan, who used her lilting voice to bring life to this Appalachian folk song. The word "on'ry" or "ornery," its usual spelling, is described by the Merriam-Webster dictionary as "having an irritable disposition." I've been noticing a lot of irritability across our entire society, and often in my own corner of the world, including within my mind. But the hymn states the promise that Jesus came for us poor on'ry people like you and me. So, could that be the answer to our world's current state of chaos? Of all the things you could wonder about today, pause to stand in awe under the big sky we all share and give thanks for that promise.

Your Turn

1. What is your favorite word? What about this word makes it your favorite? Look up the definition online or in a dictionary (if you still have one!). Write it down. Did you discover anything new, and does it change your perception of this word?

2. Where are you seeing irritability in your life? Draw a clock face on a piece of paper and keep it handy throughout the day. Circle the hours when you seem to be most irritable. Do you see a way that taking time to wonder and wander could bring calm and peace? Try taking a meditative walk sometime this week—no phone, no distractions. Pay attention to what's around you, listen, and see how taking in the world more actively changes the rest of your day.

3. What do you have yet to create in your life? A handcrafted project? A new experience? Is it something about which you could say, "This is one of the best things I've ever done in my life"? Tell a friend your idea and ask him or her to keep you accountable for making it happen!

Chapter Nine

Fear or Trust

"You'll never find a rainbow if you're looking down."
Charlie Chaplin

My first formal learning experience was swimming lessons. I was five years old. I still get shivers thinking of how scared I was to get in the water. I would sit on the edge of the pool dangling my feet in the chilly water, head tucked down, and avoiding eye contact with my teacher. I can still feel the nubby fabric of my aquamarine one-piece swimming suit getting caught on the rough concrete surface as I squirmed nervously. We were supposed to be jumping in, but I didn't want to. There were other kids my age splashing around and confidently dunking their heads under the water. I would have happily stayed home, but then I wouldn't get that peanut butter Chick-O-Stick at the end of my lesson, and my older sisters would certainly have called me a scaredy-cat. That fear of the water I felt as a five-year-old eventually subsided. By the time I was in fifth grade, I was diving off the high diving board in that same pool. I don't recall exactly when the fear went away. I'm sure it didn't happen overnight; it was a process.

Wouldn't it be great if fear were something one grows out of, kind of like ear infections or a penchant for sour gummy worms? I have certainly felt fear during these years prior to my sixtieth birthday. At age fifty-seven, I made the jump to retirement from my nursing career. Even though I had already been working part-time and was spending many hours a week volunteering, it was hard to give up that professional role and title. I mean, I had no idea what to say when people asked me, "What do you do?" I felt fear several years earlier, too, when I sat with my father, who was in and out of ICU for twenty-eight days before the words "well done, good and faithful servant" welcomed him to his heavenly home.

At both of those times, I found solace in writing. Writing had been a favorite hobby during middle school and high school, and I decided that I had something to say. It was scary, but I was blessed to have a strong mentor who gave me valuable feedback, both positive and negative. She had already authored her own blog, published a book, and started an inspiring non-profit called Breathe Bravely. If I had been asked to predict who would be a mentor to me at this stage in my life, I wouldn't have expected to name a woman only thirty years old. I don't know if I chose her or if she chose me, but I wouldn't trade our relationship for anything. Why? Because she is brave and speaks clearly and honestly.

Ashley Ballou-Bonnema lives bravely and thrives each day with cystic fibrosis (CF). She lives with a disease that could easily allow her to fixate on her medication regime and lung function numbers, but she chooses to focus on other people. She has used her gifts of teaching and music to improve the quality of life for those living with CF. Her influence as a mentor and friend has changed my perspective on aging, authenticity, gratitude, and fear. A few years ago, she faced her fear of people knowing about her CF. She describes that life-changing choice this way:

"In order to live in the freedom of truth, one must bravely embrace one's authentic self—it's only in that truth do we know the gift of what it means to truly live. As I wrestled with the decision of whether to open up about my life with CF, I knew the more I tried to run from it, the more I felt it was gaining on me. Suffocating me. Drowning me. Instead of running, I knew I had to simply turn and embrace it, freeing myself from the chains of perceived impossibilities. And, by doing so, I gave myself the permission to wholly be myself and live a life reflecting the beauty and goodness that is poured into me by all that surrounds me."

How does it look for you? Are you already in the swimming pool and learning new strokes or are you curled up on the side of the pool, shivering at the thought of your third act? That image of being turned in on oneself is a perfect depiction of fear, for me. You are looking inside yourself for power and strength when, in fact, you need to be turning your gaze out towards others.

Have you ever had an issue that has consumed you and you can't stop worrying about it, so you phone a friend to let it all out? The simple yet brave act of sharing your story seems to dissipate the anxiety, deflating its space in your mind and heart. It feels good to turn your ear to a friend's words of hope and encouragement, rather than listening to that drone of insecurity coming from your own head; it is a prescription for the relief of fear. I'm not exactly sure how I eventually got into the pool that first time, but I'm sure it had something to do with the people who were already in the water.

What would you do today if you weren't afraid? I'd probably schedule that mammogram or colonoscopy, but my fear of bad news or a bad diagnosis is very real. Just typing it now makes it sound *so* silly: I'm a nurse, or I used to be. What's on your fear list? Retiring? Taking a trip? Reuniting with a family member? Dropping a bad habit? Going out on a date? Be mindful of what God puts in front of you. Turn toward those things and not back into yourself—yes, often easier said than done.

If I were to ask you what is the opposite of fear, what words would you choose? Maybe courage, trust, acceptance, confidence, or calm—all of the above? Martin Marty is a pastor who wrote a thoughtful book about the Sermon on the Mount given by Jesus to his disciples as they rested, found in Matthew chapters five through seven. The book by Marty is titled *Speaking of Trust: Conversing with Luther about the Sermon on the Mount.* [1] You may be familiar with the cadence of the opening lines of that sermon, which begins, "Blessed are the poor in spirit for theirs is the kingdom of heaven," and continues with a litany of heartache and hope. Which words of the sermon resonate with you today—"mourn," "meek," "hunger," "thirst," "merciful," "peacemaker," "pure in heart," "persecuted"? Accepting rather than fearing that these conditions and roles will come to us, especially in our third act of life, will strengthen us for whatever comes our way. In the Lord's Prayer, we say, "Thy kingdom come, thy will be done, on earth as it is in heaven." Look up; the kingdom of heaven is yours, right now. Let that mysterious, calming promise wash over you and remove the fear. You truly are blessed.

Marty goes on to imagine a walk through the meadow where the flowers are blooming and the birds are flitting. Hear these words from the Sermon on the Mount from Matthew 6: 26–27: "Look at the birds of the air; they do not sow or reap or store away in barns, and yet your heavenly Father feeds them. Are you not much more valuable than they? Can any one of us by worrying add a single hour to our life?"

I love both Martin Luther's and Martin Marty's take on this. Luther points out that we have "as many teachers and preachers as there are little birds in the air." [1] They preach to us about the joy of life when one trusts that the Lord will provide. It's as if they are saying, "I sing and frolic, and yet I do not know of a single grain that I am to eat. My bread is not baked yet, and my grain is not planted yet." Can you imagine living this way? The key is in these words, "Are you not much more valuable than they?" It's true. We are His children, and we are much more valued than the birds. Let these words empower you to be more trusting and more carefree than you were yesterday. You may have to be reminded again tomorrow, but no worries; the promises are always there.

Your Turn

1. One of my favorite nursing professors, Dr. Joyce Nelson, taught me that there is a thin line between the emotions of fear and anger. Have you experienced this? Describe a time that you were angry but, deep down, you were actually scared.

2. List three things you would do today if you weren't afraid. Share these with a friend and challenge them to share a similar list. Support each other in overcoming what scares each of you and stepping out in faith.

3. Consider how much time you spend thinking about the past, the present, and the future. Draw a circle with lines indicating your thinking time in three sections—one labeled past, one present, one future. Which section is the largest, which is the smallest? How would you like your sections to be balanced?

Chapter Ten

Invisible

> "I don't need a cloak to become invisible."
> **J.K. Rowling, *Harry Potter and the Sorcerer's Stone***

My dad, Juel, was a kind and jolly man. I wrote earlier about his last words to me shortly before he died, which were, "Don't take life too seriously." As poignant and powerful as that moment was, this was not a new message for me. Being raised by him and my more serious mom on a farm in rural South Dakota, I benefited from the joy he brought to life—even in the most ordinary of days. Dad was the one who put us to bed and cooked us scrambled eggs in the morning. My mom was a high school English teacher and would be correcting papers when it was time for us to go to bed, so bedtime was Dad time.

Our bedtime routine with Dad included a rousing game of hide-and-seek in the upstairs of our farmhouse. There were four of us kids and a tiny upstairs. I'm sure we repeated many of the same hiding places, but my dad made it an adventure nonetheless. I can picture going into my parents' bedroom closet, stepping on my mom's high-heeled shoes and pushing my way past her collection of dresses to get into the back corner piled high with empty shoeboxes. Then, the most important part, I stayed completely silent and listened excitedly for his call, "Ready or not, here I come!" I was sure I was invisible. On the nights he found me, he tickled me until I cried, "Uncle!" Then he tossed me into my creaky old metal bed. But on some nights, he just couldn't find me. He would give up the hunt, and I would hear him yell, "Ollie, ollie, oxen free," which was code for, "Come back, you're free!" Then, my siblings and I would quickly crawl out of our hiding places and tickle my dad.

At this stage in my life, I have found that I don't need to play hide and seek to make myself invisible. It just seems to happen naturally. Perception is reality, and at times I perceive that I go unnoticed or unheard. I know I am not alone in this phenomenon. Invisibility can happen in my own house, when I am ignored by my husband, whom I adore, or it can happen in a more public setting. A few months ago, I was seated at a large square table of sixteen people at our tasting room in the Napa Valley. We were doing some strategizing about our wine sales, and I made a comment that I thought was quite pertinent. Not one person acknowledged my statement. A few seconds later, a male counterpart said the exact same thing, and the whole table agreed with him and gave him adulation for his insight. I don't think they didn't *hear* me, but they certainly didn't *listen* to me. On another occasion, I was serving a twelve-year stint on a board, which I loved, providing strong leadership and mission-driven direction. Completing a private exit interview for one of our outgoing board members, my colleague stated, "Becky, you have been a ray of sunshine on the board." I accepted the compliment, of course, but left feeling quite deflated. That's what I've been doing all these years? Serving as a ray of sunshine? Maybe it's time for those of us in our third act to turn up the heat.

One Fourth of July weekend, I experienced one of those "Holy Spirit turning my head" sort of moments when I heard the call of my neighbor in the lobby of our church following the worship service. This longtime sister in Christ began sharing her holiday weekend experience of hosting her family at their lake home. The story included unfortunate family interactions and behaviors—leaving my friend feeling disrespected, unappreciated, and ultimately, in her words, "invisible." It was evident that this situation was painful, leaving scars that she hoped would heal. Neither of us are shrinking violets, and our shared experience of feeling invisible was both frustrating and thought provoking.

Type "I feel invisible" into your Google search bar and you will get 200 million results. It's a thing. I randomly clicked on "4 Ways You're Making Yourself Invisible"—which suggests we are to blame. The link led me to a site where author and relationship expert Dr. Margaret Paul lists four culprits. First, if you ignore your own feelings, it's easy for others to ignore them, too. Wow, let that sink in—*if you ignore your own feelings, it's easy for others to ignore them, too*. Second, if you don't advocate for yourself, no one else will; by being silent when we are hurt or mistreated, others have no need to respond to us. Third, accepting one-way relationships—always hearing friends, family, and coworkers talk about themselves but never hearing them ask about you—can be a green light for them to ignore you. Fourth, being a people-pleaser. On this final point, Dr. Paul writes: "If you're trying to gain others' approval by being nice, then your niceness is a form of control and will likely backfire." She goes on to explain that "people don't like to be controlled, and they can easily pick up the energy of a controlling agenda. The result might be that they withdraw and ignore you—the exact opposite of what you want." [1]

As a nurse trained in psychology, I agree with Dr. Paul's advice. But as a nurse who is also a person of faith, I offer another perspective. She uses lots of "you, your, yourself" language or, in another voice, "me, myself, I." These pronouns are the foundation of turning in on oneself. How do those internal messages and, subsequently, our perspective change if we uncurl ourselves and turn our eyes upward and outward?

I have a small book I bought years ago at a Women of Faith conference. The book, written by Nicole Johnson, is titled *The Invisible Woman: When Only God Sees*. [2] I recall being mesmerized at the conference watching the author role play what it is like to be a mom—the demands, the chaos, the selflessness, the invisibility. At the time, I was a young mom myself and could completely relate to her vignettes of being unseen and unheard by her children and her husband. She writes in her book, "The more I poured myself into my family, the more invisible I became." Now as I reread the book fifteen years later, I still find it relatable. Johnson invokes images of the great cathedrals of Europe, asking the reader to imagine walking inside one of these expansive spaces, footsteps echoing in the aisle, and then turning your head to the ceiling high above you. What would you see? You might see the intricate carvings on the arches, the colorful stained-glass windows, and the gold leaf framing the voluminous dome above the altar. What would you not see? There are no names of the craftsmen, tile setters, carvers, and painters. They are invisible, but their work has been visible for centuries. They persevered each day because they knew they were part of something beyond themselves, even though they may never get to see the finished cathedral in their lifetime.

She comes to this conclusion: "Invisibility is no longer a disease that is erasing my life. It is actually the hard cure for the disease of self-centeredness."[2] Could the fix for invisibility be to turn our gaze outward and upward, toward our neighbor and our God? I've been working on this in my own life, and I can honestly say that the days when I look up and out are better than the days I look down and in. When I feel unheard in a meeting or ignored by friends or taken for granted by my family, it really doesn't matter because I believe God sees me. That belief brings a promise and a lightness of being that moves me through my day and turns me to where I am needed most.

Your Turn

1. Give an example of a time when you have felt invisible. Take a few minutes to describe the experience in detail.

2. On a scale of 1 to 10, how difficult would it be for you to look up and out rather than looking down and in? What could make it easier?

3. Describe your perfect sanctuary. Write words that describe it or sketch a scene. Add the date so that you can look back and see how your perspective has changed.

Chapter Eleven

Let Yourself Be Surprised!

"What we plan for is not as satisfying as what comes
by chance and through divine generosity."
Martin Marty

I began 2020 with my predictable end-of January pattern of
taking down my Christmas tree (I leave our tree up until the
end of January so I can enjoy the lights during our dark and cold
evenings) and writing my Christmas cards—not necessarily in
that order. February was a bunch of fun as we celebrated in the
Napa Valley with our winery crew—a fantastic "Roaring Twenties" themed holiday party. We then headed to New Zealand
for three weeks, where we visited health clinics throughout
the country as part of my husband's work. I think our travels

took us to twenty-five clinics requiring at least eight in-country flights. We flew home March 1, ready to do all the things that our calendar said we would be doing. We were living in the roaring twenties! Then ... well, you know what happened then. The world turned upside down. As I write this, we have made it to July 2020 of the coronavirus pandemic but with really no end in sight. I think we could all use some of that divine generosity that Pastor Martin Marty is referring to in the opening quote to this chapter. For months, I have been teetering between thankfulness for good health and an insistence that I'm sure I have the virus. I guess I'm not alone in this.

This year has been full of surprises. Personally, a big one came during May when my husband, Dan, learned that he would be retiring—about three years earlier than he had planned. Of course, my first thought was that old joke, "I married you for better or for worse, but not for lunch!" Then I turned out of myself, and for the past three months have been asking him, "Are you doing okay?" The answer varies from day to day. Honestly, what could be better for a writer who's writing about the magic and mystery of more days than having her partner go through the retirement transition in real time? Let me get my notepad!

The official retirement happened two weeks ago. So far, my best way to describe Dan is a corn popper with the lid off. One of my longtime nursing colleagues and I developed a personality inventory based on which appliance you are—a popcorn popper or crockpot. She was always the popcorn popper, and I was always the crockpot. I diagnosed my husband's condition immediately—immediately for a crockpot, that is, i.e., in eight to ten hours on low. Each day—no, each hour—he has a different plan, a different mood, a different regret, a different gratefulness. To add to the uncertainty, he had to go to his annual physical on his first day of retirement! Thankfully, he was given a clean bill of health.

I'm officially calling our current situation a *transition*, which I know can trip people up or stop them in their tracks. William Bridges, author of *Transitions: Making Sense of Life Changes* was the transition guru in the 1980s, coaching people through divorce, death of a parent, or the birth of a child. The cornerstone of his work was to frame each transition and each part of a transition with honor. He names three parts of a transition: endings, the neutral zone or "time of fertile emptiness," and new beginnings. In his words, "Transitions clear the ground for new growth." That needs to be on a sticky note on our refrigerator.

Bridges developed a transition checklist[1], which should also be on our fridge, and maybe yours? He suggests the following:

- Take your time. Our outer life can change in an instant, but our inner life needs time to reorient.
- Arrange temporary structures. Create ways of going on with life while you are doing the hard work of transition—rediscovering an old hobby, accepting a part-time job or volunteer opportunity to fill some of the holes.

- Don't act for the sake of action. We need time to bring closure to our last adventure and assess what we learned prior to going ahead to the next one.
- Recognize why you are uncomfortable. Distress is not necessarily a sign that something has gone wrong, but rather that something is changing.
- Take care of yourself in little ways. This is probably not the time for an extreme makeover, but do take care of yourself, treat yourself.
- Explore the other side of change. Think of the possibilities ahead, as you still might be missing or mourning your previous work.
- Get someone to talk to. Find a good listener rather than an advice giver.
- Find out what is waiting in the wings of your life. In Bridges' words, "What is it at this point in your life that is waiting quietly backstage for an entrance cue?"
- Use this transition as an impetus to a new kind of learning. What do you need to learn for a new opportunity?
- Recognize that transition has a characteristic shape. Things end, there is a time of fertile emptiness, and then things begin anew.

My friend, Lon Kightlinger, served years as a state epidemiologist before he retired and immediately moved to Madagascar to serve in the Peace Corps. This was a full circle move for Lon, as this is where he had first worked as a young college graduate, but he knew that things would be different this time around. I asked him what the surprises have been. First, he said, "I'm surprised I had the chutzpah and fortitude to not just idealize Peace Corps service, but actually do it." Second, he has been both surprised and impressed by his adaptability: "I'm living in two tiny rooms at the rural health center. No running water, using an outhouse toilet, sweltering heat, noisy neighbors, loud roosters, mosquito bed nets, cockroaches, hand washing my laundry, open sewers, and the mud ... none of these have bothered me too much. Whereas back in the USA, I'm sure I would be complaining to the city council, my pastor, or even the governor." Lon spends his days with coworkers who are mostly in their twenties. He is surprised at the unexpected friendships that have developed, and only a few times he has heard them say, "You sound just like my dad." He proudly reports, "They even accepted me into the Peace Corps Millennial Club!"

My favorite question to ask during my geriatric nursing practice was, "How old do you feel right now?" When I asked Lon, he quickly answered, "I feel like I'm thirty-three years old—optimistic and idealistic. But when I look at the skin on my hands or catch my reflection in the mirror, and feel bedtime calling at 9:00 p.m., I realize I am double that age. My youthful optimism, idealism, and innocence are now tempered by experience, reality, disappointments, heartbreak, loss, cynicism, and fuddy-duddyisms. I am thankful for the many blessings and opportunities I have had during my life and only wish I could pass those graces on to others. I am always amused to write or click '1952' as my birth year. Who me? Can't be."

Now that both Dan and I have arrived at that mile marker called retirement, I am beginning to feel and understand what Paul Irving stated bluntly in his book, *The Upside of Aging: How Long Life is Changing the World of Health, Work, Innovation, Policy, and Purpose.* He writes, "The whole issue of retirement is increasingly irrelevant, or at least less important, when we see our lives as a continuum of interwoven threads that blend and intersect unpredictably."[2]

I believe the important choice is to not turn in on ourselves but to turn outward and keep our ears open to those words of promise "for you" that Jesus speaks. Remember that a promise doesn't depend on the person receiving it, but rather on the one who gives it. Life will be abundant and full of surprises. You can take that to the bank, as my dad would say.

I fondly recall the best advice my son was given as he graduated from high school. A wise cousin, Ingrid, who knew him well, simply stated, "Be open to the possibilities!" I see this stage in our life as a commencement of sorts. We don't need any gifts, but we do need the openness and the freedom that is encouraged in our younger counterparts. I often tell graduates, "Go and find your people! Picture yourself in that new place—and always be open to the adventures that God puts before you."

Like many young people leaving high school or college, some retirees are now taking a "gap year" between retirement and whatever comes next to explore all the possibilities.

Of course, this will look different than a younger person's gap year due to many variables that probably don't exist for most eighteen-year-olds, such as family and financial commitments, caregiving duties, health needs, and housing. However, don't let these variables become barriers to turning your gaze towards the rest of your life and letting yourself be surprised. You may not do a gap year, but maybe you'll find an art class, a local nonprofit, or a political cause that draws you in and helps you sketch new ways of being in your third act. I see that in my neighbor, Steve, who each day can be found walking a different dog from the local humane society. He sometimes yells, "Hi Becky, stay away from this one!" We aren't all looking for a third act that's full of puppies and rainbows, but we still want to be challenged and to give back.

Your Turn

1. Draw a rectangle that you can pretend is a stage. What at this point in your life is waiting quietly backstage for an entrance cue? Write those words outside the rectangle and save your drawing for frequent viewing.

2. In what ways do you hope to be surprised in your next decade? Pose this question the next time you're gathered around a table of friends.

3. Could you see yourself taking a "gap year"? How would you spend that time, and with whom? Would it include service, learning, writing, travel, hobbies, or something else? Where would you go? Write down five things you'd like to fill your ideal gap year with.

Chapter Twelve

Grief and Loss

"There is no grief like the grief that does not speak."
Henry Wadsworth Longfellow

The soundtrack of my childhood was Carole King's *Tapestry* album. We had a quirky octagon-shaped side table in our farmhouse living room, next to our green crushed-velvet couch. It hid a record player inside that my sisters and I would use often. I think I can still sing every line of the *Tapestry* album. During my high school years, when my mom was ill with cancer, that turntable turned our hearts and ears to something joyful and distracting.

A few years ago, we took a family vacation to New York City. One evening, we headed to Broadway for a recently opened show—*Beautiful: The Carole King Musical.* I loved every minute of the show, but once the curtain closed, I started crying buckets. Luckily, my daughter was next to me and stood guard over my feelings. It was as if a cork that had kept years and years of grief and loss over my mom's death had been pried out of me with each familiar chorus and verse. I had cried over her loss before, and I can still recall some of those poignant moments, but this particular outpouring was unexpected. A time to dance, a time to mourn ... turn, turn, turn.

Grief and loss are commonalities of the human condition, and these experiences naturally increase with age. I experienced my mom's death when I was sixteen, and it gave me a perspective that I carried throughout my nursing practice and my personal life. I watched as she gradually withered away at the end of her life. I will never forget the Monday night before she died. My dad returned from visiting her at the hospital. He curled up on our green crushed-velvet couch, looked at each of us kids perched around the room, and spoke words I will never forget, "I don't think your mom is coming home, kids." It was something I had suspected but didn't really believe until I heard him say those words on that night. Her death on the following Friday evening certainly prepared me for subsequent losses, including the deaths of grandparents, friends, and the loss of my dad twelve years ago at the age of eighty-three. For me, there has been a resiliency that comes with the lived experience of loss, even though the grief never really leaves. For me, grief has mellowed over time, kind of like the aging of a fine wine. The more we love, the more we will have opportunities to grieve.

Connor Gwin, an Episcopal chaplain and blogger, lost his mom while he was a child and his dad as a graduate student. He acknowledges becoming somewhat of a grief expert from his lived experiences. He writes in his blog posted on *Mockingbird*: "Here is the problem: grieving never stops. The human condition is to grieve. We grieve our childhood, our family of origin, our hometown, our dreams for our lives, our significant other that got away, our former (thinner) self. We grieve our plans for the day as a child wakes up with a fever. We grieve our shattered expectations for our lives. To be human is to grieve. We are all grieving all the time, but we work to convince ourselves that everything is fine. We put in more hours at the office, we reorganize the closet again, we start training for the full marathon this time. We keep busy so that we don't have to sit still long enough to realize that we are awash with grief." [1]

One of the best choices my husband and I have made together was to say yes to an invitation to join a couples' Bible study about fifteen years ago. Those years spent with the same four couples two Sunday evenings a month were fun and formative for enduring friendships and lively faith discussions. One of the husbands, Monte, had the driest wit and an amazing way of distilling clarity out of the ten-way chatter. It probably helped that he was an attorney, but he could have easily been a stand-up comedian. We all loved Monte. Tragically, Monte's chronic illnesses compounded, and he died toward the end of our Bible-study run. His beautiful wife, Vicki, often reflects on her grief since that day in March six years ago when we gathered round his hospital bed and sang hymns to send him off to heaven.

Now, six years later, Vicki has a rich store of wisdom about her grief journey that she willingly shares. First, she is quick to admit that grief is a personal journey. As much as she wanted to rely on her high-school psychology knowledge of Elisabeth Küblar-Ross's stages of grief, it was different for her: "There is no map. No timeline. It's so fluid." She says, "To me grief is like being surrounded by a circle, and all these arrows of grief were penetrating every part of my world ... but as I grieved, it was as if a cushion of other voices formed outside the circle. The grief is still there, no less piercing, but cushioned by new experiences and new people." She is so grateful to those who helped her grieve. She says the thing that surprised her most after Monte's death was the impact his death had on other people—friends and coworkers: "They were grieving right alongside me, and that was comforting. I loved when they would say, 'I miss him, too.'" She welcomed people talking about Monte—and still does. She reminds them, "You're not adding to the sadness."

Vicki says, "I think you have to embrace the grief and let it be part of your life. Honestly, it's almost become a comfort to me. I still hear Monte often in my mind; he reminds me what's most important in life." She admits to having a lot less fear than she ever did before: "I hold that promise that we'll be together again—not in a physical sense but in a soul way." Vicki knows that the grief doesn't leave and neither does the promise that we are held by God.

Dr. Ken Jones, theology professor at Grandview University in Des Moines—and back in the day my camp counselor buddy at Outlaw Ranch—weighed in on grief during a recent visit:

"Here's why we grieve: We put our faith in the law. We believe we can harness life and concoct a future through our own efforts and exertions of the will. Then we become our own agents. And we'll always be disappointed, because the only way to achieve what we want is via absolute control of every possible element that creates that future. So, God, who does have a finger on every lever, lets the grieving and loss begin. It's like Luther said: 'Only when we completely despair of ourselves can we merit the mercy of Christ.' Only then, when our fingers are pried from the steering wheel, can life become a gift—and a joyous surprise. It's one of the best things about getting to the third act of life. Nothing HAS to happen. Except that it all has to happen because it's structured and ordered by the God of limitless mercy and grace."

That recognition and release that it "all has to happen" allows for the awareness of so many God-ordained magical moments. I have a small gesture that I like to do when someone has experienced the death of a loved one or is standing watch over someone in his or her last days. I give them the book *Final Gifts: Understanding the Special Awareness, Needs, and Communications of the Dying.*[2] The authors, Maggie Callanan and Patricia Kelley, are hospice nurses with years of experience in caring for the dying. I give the book with instructions to be on the watch for final gifts that their loved one will give them, both before and after passing. It might be last words like my dad's ("Don't take life too seriously") that become a life lesson for grandchildren today. It could be my red shrub roses that bloom on each of our children's graduation days as a gift from my mom. It might be a last handwritten letter to a sixteen-year-old daughter away at camp that closes with the simple words, "Well, have a good time and do all you can to be someone or learn something." Look for the final gifts, write them down, tuck them away, and claim them as yours.

Your Turn

1. Are you grieving today? Using my friend Vicki's descriptions of her grief, draw a circle with you in the middle. Draw arrows pointing towards the circle and label each with a word that states what you are grieving or what you have lost. Can you write words between you and the arrows that describe what is cushioning you now from your grief or what you are hoping to have cushion you?

2. What have you learned about grief that you could teach someone else? Write one sentence that includes your wisdom. Consider someone you might share it with who is experiencing grief.

3. Have you received any final gifts from a friend or family member just before or after their death? What were they, and did they help with your grief?

Chapter Thirteen

Sketching Joy

"In spite of everything I shall rise again: I will take up my pencil, which I have forsaken in my great discouragement, and I will go on with my drawing."
Vincent van Gogh

If you haven't experienced the children's book *Harold and the Purple Crayon*, it comes recommended by my thirty-one-year-old son, Ian, and me. It's one of the favorites that I had read countless times to Ian because it truly is the perfect bedtime story—short and full of imagination to send the liveliest of children off to la-la land. As I reread it today, I experienced it in a new way. In fact, I think it could be rebranded as the perfect sixtieth birthday gift. The gist of the story is that little Harold, a curious and creative boy, takes his purple crayon and draws his life. At the beginning of the story, he sneaks out of his bedroom into the night: "He made a long, straight path so he wouldn't get lost. And he set off on his walk, taking his big purple crayon with him. But he didn't seem to be getting anywhere on the long, straight path. So, he left the path for a shortcut across the field. And the moon went with him." [1]

As I flipped through the book, I noticed that the moon is on every page. Harold hasn't drawn the moon into each of those scenes; he draws the picnic, and the pies, and the sky-scrapers, but the moon is always there. I suppose you've caught on to my object lesson by now. Yes, I now see the moon as God, Jesus, and the Holy Spirit. Near the end of the book, after drawing a variety of adventures, Harold turns his head upward, spies the bright beacon, and he walks "along with the moon." Maybe our third act is that simple: to let a figurative purple crayon sketch what comes next as we walk along with Jesus.

A friend of mine, Bob, was fifty-eight and CEO of the company his father established and grew from scratch. In Bob's words, he was "at the apex of my commercial career." His financial position gave him great freedom. "I no longer needed to work, so I was increasingly drawn to the concerns of my relationship with God." He served in a leadership role in his church, which one day gave him the opportunity to have lunch with a Lutheran theologian. The conversation included controversies in the church and, in Bob's words, "theological food fights." That lunch was the beginning of a call that ultimately led Bob to leave his career and spend the next several years attending seminary. "My wife, friends, and family were as stunned as I was. I've not regretted my decision for a single moment. Has it all worked out as I anticipated? Not at all. My career in parish work was short (two years), but I have served my Lord and Savior in many different ministries and other unexpected ways. At the core of it all is a deep satisfaction that I've come to a much clearer understanding of how to live the joyful, abundant life that Christ promises."

Sometimes, joy magically begins with sketches on a paper napkin. My husband's family is famous for this—usually at coffee time or as a post-dinner activity—someone will smooth out a paper napkin, ask for a pen, and start sketching. Months later, the sketch turns into an actual suspension bridge in our backyard! My father-in-law had been sketching an addition to their house with the goal of creating a master bedroom on the main floor and, in his words, "To give Barb the kitchen she has always wanted." My father-in-law is eighty-seven and my mother-in-law is eighty-six. There is no expiration date on sketching! There is surely no expiration date on making those drawings come alive and create a new life—just as Harold did. Appropriately, author Crockett Johnson wrote and illustrated *Harold and the Purple Crayon* in 1955—the year that my in-laws were married.

Paul Klee, a German-Swiss artist from the early nineteen-hundreds, stated, "A drawing is simply a line going for a walk." If we think certain activities in our third act of life are too difficult or too atypical, maybe we just need to put them to paper. Simply draw them, write them down, look at them, and speak them in words to someone across a table over a cup of coffee. I remember how long it took me to share with people closest to me that I wanted to write a book about turning sixty. Once I said it out loud, it magically became more possible, and the encouragement from friends and family were reminders that I was going to do it. It's almost been a year since I started writing, and sometimes I've "dropped my crayon" for weeks before refocusing and getting back at it. I will count it all as joy.

An update on that house remodel—it's happening! The kitchen remodel is finished, and my mother-in-law just went shopping for a full set of pots and pans for her new range. The bedroom build is beginning, under the keen eye of the general contractor—my father-in-law, an adult version of Harold. Each time we speak on the phone you can hear the joy in their voices as they see their newest story coming to life. Makes me want to pick up my crayon.

Your Turn

1. Clear your voice from your head with some words from God. Say a prayer or read some scripture. Hear these words from Romans 15:13: "May the God of hope fill you with all joy and peace as you trust in him, so that you may overflow with hope by the power of the Holy Spirit." Now draw a picture of where a purple crayon powered by the Holy Spirit wants to take you.

2. Do you hold your imaginary crayon loosely, like Harold does in the story, and see which way you turn, or do you grip it tightly, keeping control of your next move? Or would you rather not even have a crayon?

3. Next time you're shopping, pick up a box of crayons and keep the purple one—or any color—on your desk as a reminder to keep turning to new callings. Who would you like to give a purple crayon to? Why? How might a purple crayon change their life?

Chapter Fourteen

Flowers and
Wild Forgiveness

"Once a woman has forgiven her man, she must not reheat
his sins for breakfast."
Marlene Dietrich

My first garden was lovingly designed by my husband. I still have
the pencil drawing of the vegetable plots carefully sketched by Dan
and given to me as a Mother's Day gift. I loved the design of the tall
central beanpole and the triangular beds that branched out from it
that would nurture the carrot, radish, and spinach seeds, and the
tomato plants. Not only did he draw the garden plan, but he helped
me plant it and, ultimately, did most of the weeding. (I always like
projects when they're new—then my interest and attention wanes.)
I added an additional feature to the garden. I planted a long row of

cosmos seeds the full thirty-foot length of the garden bed. If you aren't familiar with cosmos, they have tall, leggy, feathery green stems that hold simple, bright blooms in all shades of pink. The day that now lives in infamy in our marriage is the day these tall feathery stems were just ready to burst forth from their green buds. I still recall driving up to our house after work and seeing Dan bent over the cosmos pulling them out from the roots. Near him was a pile at least six feet tall of my cosmos plants. When I screamed at him asking what he was doing he screamed back, "I thought they were weeds!" I was horrified and so angry. I'm not sure I've ever truly forgiven him, and I've reheated that story plenty of times.

I haven't completely given up on flowers. Today my back is sore because I've been in my front garden, bent over doing a necessary, tedious, and yet oddly satisfying task. I was "deadheading" the flowers. It is the middle of July, and I'm sure I planted the daisies in their pots sometime around Mother's Day, so it's about time. I love white flowers against the red brick of our house, so I chose white Shasta daisies, white wave petunias, silvery dusty miller, and vinca vine for some green. I guess I've been able to appreciate the beautiful fresh blooms without noticing the dried-up daisies standing in bold, brown contrast. Can we all agree that petunias are the lowest maintenance flower that God created? Deadheading them is child's play—like picking up a Cheerio off the floor. Now, the daisies; they're ornery. They like to stay put. They stand tall and act as if no one can even see them. They think they are hiding—but today I noticed them. I slid on my dirty garden gloves, grabbed the small pruning shears, and went to work. One by one, I clipped each shriveled bloom and dropped it in my bucket. The more I cut, the more I seemed to find. The more I cut, the more beautiful the entire flowerpot became. I consider myself an average gardener at best, but I do know that pruning will stimulate new growth and longer lasting blooms.

Forgiving someone, or yourself, is often a deadheading task. Some hurtful actions can be easily blown off rather quickly, kind of like deadheading a petunia. This might be forgiving your daughter who hasn't called in weeks or forgiving your husband for forgetting your weekend plans. Other hurtful actions are harder to let go of; they stand sturdy on the top of your mind and heart like those dried-up daisies. To get rid of them takes a good hard pull or the pruning shears; sometimes, honestly, it's just easier to ignore them and leave them there.

Have you ever experienced a deceitful relationship, a dishonest business deal, or maybe the personal disappointment of not making a good decision? What were once bright blooms in your life sometimes become dark, dry, hard spots. They can re-emerge as resentment, anger, hatred, and all the other physical symptoms that can accompany those mental weights— sleeplessness, emotional eating, depression, and many others. These feelings and actions are normal, but not life giving. So, what's a good gardener to do? After plenty of trial and error, I have found that going to the master creator who makes all things new is the right next step. The old adage of "forgive and forget" may have been gleaned from these words from the prophet Isaiah: "Forget the former things; do not dwell on the past. See, I am doing a new thing! Now it springs up, do you not perceive it? I am making a way in the wilderness and streams in the wasteland." (Isaiah 43:18–19). The "new thing" for us each day is a new identity in Christ Jesus. The promise that we are forgiven by Jesus allows us to turn and forgive others. There will be days when people and things you love are pulled up from the roots. You will be left feeling angry and powerless, maybe even hopeless. Know that God is making a way for you through the wilderness, doing all the gardening, and creating new blooms as far as your eye can see. God is all about wild forgiveness. That is the gospel.

A recent hike on the gravel paths through the forest near Breckenridge, Colorado, illustrated the wild gardening that our creator does. Those daisies I fussed about at my house were thriving in the wild. Some were in large, intertwined clumps. Some were single stems erupting from beneath a rock. All were brightly blooming. There were bluebells and lupine bursting freely along the path, bringing joy to this thankful hiker. It reminded me that my daily walk through life might be much different if I let God do the pruning of my burdens. Because of God's promise through Jesus Christ, I can be perfectly passive. I like how theologian Rev. Dr. Steve Paulson described this promise so simply and elegantly in a recent Luther House podcast:

"I am here. You are mine. Watch what happens." [1]

Your Turn

1. Sketch a blooming flowerpot. What are the blooms that bring joy to you today? Are there dried-up blooms or burdens that need to be pruned? Is it pruning that only God can do?

2. Sketch a garden plot. Instead of vegetables, mark the relationships or adventures that you would like to grow and nurture in your next decade of life. Write the date on your sketch and revisit it often.

3. What has God planted before you today that only requires you to turn and give thanks?

Chapter Fifteen

Daily Bread and Butter

"You are the butter to my bread, and the breath to my life."

Julia Child

At our Handwritten Wines tasting room in Yountville, California, we offer a delicious experience to our customers. It is a bread-and-butter tasting. Read that again: a bread-and-butter tasting. It could be called a "manna from heaven tasting"— that's how beautiful it sounds and truly how nourishing it is. Picture sitting around an antique farm table with one, two, or six of your best friends and drinking elegant wine paired with crusty bread from the Bouchon Bakery down the street. On the table are four silver dishes, each containing a different butter from around the world. As our wine educator leads you through the variety of cabernet sauvignons, you are encouraged to slather the butter on the bread and experience the nuances of each one. During this tasting, you completely tune in to your other senses of sight, smell, sound, and even touch. While your mouth is filled with tasty bread and wine, your ears are filled with the conversations of your companions and the teachings from our staff; you are being fed in many ways. After a couple of hours, which have passed too quickly, you take some final photos, thank the gracious staff, and walk out into the world, surely with a glad heart, a big smile, and possibly a tad tipsy.

"Give us this day our daily bread" are words of the Lord's Prayer that have been spoken by generations of Jesus's followers since it was first recorded in the gospel of Matthew 6: 9–13, and a shorter version in the gospel of Luke 11: 2–4. I try to say this prayer each night before I fall asleep. Some nights I do better than others. It is those seven words about daily bread slipped right into the middle of the prayer that are often rushed as I push on to the "and forgive us our trespasses as we forgive those who trespass against us." I'm all about needing forgiveness and being reminded to forgive others. What if I slowed down the Lord's Prayer and dwelled on the ask, "Give us this day our daily bread"?

Our third child, Elliot, was not shy about asking for daily bread. I have a vivid memory of when he was about four years old. After saying prayers with him at bedtime he looked at me with serious eyes and said, "Mom, will you feed me tomorrow?" I assured him, "Yes, Elliot, I will feed you tomorrow." His bedtime story that night was from his children's Bible. In brightly colored drawings and simple words, it told the Old Testament story of God bringing the people of Israel manna from heaven. It showed the hungry people with long faces complaining about their journey in the desert and their fear of starving to death. Then it happened. Falling from the sky were big white flakes. With mouths wide open, the people filled their baskets with these flakes, which looked like frost on the ground and tasted like wafers made of honey. It also explained the clever twist to God's plan. Each day there was manna enough for that day, but if they tried to store it up, it would spoil. They had to trust that God would provide.

How many of us ask daily, "God, will you feed me tomorrow?" It is a centuries-old question. And we are all not just asking for food, like hungry Elliot at bedtime, we are looking for sustenance beyond the dinner table. We want the butter, the wine, the friends, the experiences. And at this stage of life, we often want to ask for more than just daily bread; we would like to ask for a year's worth, or more, as we try to align our dreams of health and travel and adventure with our finances. It's complicated, isn't it? We want to care for our neighbor, but we're not sure how much *we* need first.

Luther House of Study Director Dr. Chris Croghan, in a podcast, commented on the daily bread text in Matthew: "God delights in giving his children daily bread. We simply need to receive it and give thanks for it. It is easy to worship the created things rather than the creator. God is going to meet your needs today. Trust that—then open your hands for others to have their needs met." [1]

Be nourished today with sweet words falling, like manna, from heaven. Then use them up *today* on your children, your spouse, your neighbor, your coworker—because there will be more tomorrow.

Your Turn

1. What do you need to fall from the sky right now? What's your manna?

2. What part of your life/daily bread is it hard for you to accept freely and give thanks for?

3. On a scale of 1 to 10, how easy is it for you to share your daily bread? Are you a cheerful giver or more careful and reluctant? Consider this short story from the Gospel of Luke: *Luke 21: 1–4: The Widow's Offering.*

    "As Jesus looked up, he saw the rich putting their gifts into the temple treasury. He also saw a poor widow put in two very small copper coins. 'Truly I tell you,' he said, 'this poor widow has put in more than all the others. All these people gave their gifts out of their wealth; but she out of her poverty put in all she had to live on.'"

4. Now complete this sentence: *This month I want to share my daily bread by ...*

Chapter Sixteen

Relationships

"We are afraid to care too much, for fear that the other
person does not care at all."

Eleanor Roosevelt

I loved my days as a geriatric clinical nurse specialist. On Tuesdays, we would hold a daylong clinic and only see one patient and their family for about five hours. It was a rich professional experience being a part of an interdisciplinary team that included a geriatrician, dietician, pharmacist, social worker, physical therapist, and occupational therapist. (If you are looking for such a service in your area, search for "Geriatric Assessment Teams.") I would start the process by visiting with the client while the social worker was visiting with the family.

One of the most telling questions I would ask was, "How many people can you call on if you need help or support?" The answer varied from two or three to ten or more. Sometimes this would depend on if he or she had recently moved to the area and were just beginning to meet new people. Sometimes, though, the answer was "one"—the one being the stressed daughter who, at that moment, was visiting with the social worker. I think only once did I hear the stunning response "none."

I was in my thirties when I witnessed the power of relationships in the third act of life through the eyes of my geriatric clients. The impact of having neighbors, friends, or family upon whom one could comfortably call for a ride to the doctor or for help after a fall was nearly priceless. I am forever grateful to those struggling patients and families who shared their stories and gave me a glimpse into the reality of life after seventy, eighty, or ninety.

I was in my forties when I would watch my dad and step-mother celebrate friendships in their daily lives. My dad, from his late seventies into his eighties, would drive downtown each weekday morning to meet his coffee group in the basement of a funeral home. I'm not sure why they didn't go to the cafe just across the street—I suppose the coffee wasn't free there, and the funeral director was a great host. I think I only accompanied my dad once to his coffee group, but it was long enough to see the depth of relationships amongst the men. Old jokes about getting old, high school sports, last night's storm, and who had become the latest customer at the funeral home were daily conversation fodder. The chalkboard by the door listed each man's name and a simple line was drawn through each name when they passed away: life and death on a striking display. That daily check-in, with shared stories and a shared coffeepot, built relationships for these men. When it came time for my dad, Juel, to have his name marked with a long, thin line through it, my family was blessed by the help and support of his coffee group.

My stepmom's relationships were formed at bridge clubs and church groups. Dorothy would play bridge several times a week, and it showed in her mental acuity and ability to host a party—just put up two card tables and bake some cookies! Throughout her eighties, she continued to drive thirty-five miles to meet her bridge group and would happily report winning only two dollars. Her busy social life seemed to turn back the clock on her aging. My favorite story about her is about the time she was in the waiting room at her dentist office and seemed to be waiting longer than usual. She finally went up to the reception desk to ask why her name hadn't been called. The receptionist responded, "Well, the chart says you're eighty-six, and we couldn't see anyone that looked that old."

If I had asked Dad and Dorothy how many people they could call on for help or support, I know they could have given me a sufficient list of friends, family, and neighbors. This just doesn't happen by chance, but rather by choice. Think about that question for yourself. Let's broaden it beyond physical help. We discussed earlier that we are each whole beings, body, mind, and spirit. So, who can you call when you are hurting emotionally? Who can you call when you feel empty? Who fills your cup? Maybe your answers aren't as positive as you would have hoped for in this season of your life. Life happens. But—going back to the Ecclesiastics verse—there is a time to gain, a time to lose. Retirements, relocations, and remarriages can all change the constellation of relationships that we always thought would be there for us in our third act. We know that God is with us, but in the words of a scared little girl who calls to her mom from her bedroom at night, "I know Jesus is with me, but I want someone with skin on!" No matter our age, we are what my favorite diva Barbra Streisand sings about: "People, people who need people, are the luckiest people in the world." Yet, we can suddenly find ourselves in a situation where, if asked, we might have to admit, "Yes, I guess I'm lonely."

In his recently published book, *Together: The Healing Power of Connection in a Sometimes Lonely World,*[1] US Surgeon General Dr. Vivek Murthy speaks about loneliness. He views loneliness as a natural signal in our body, similar to hunger or thirst. Our bodies are telling us we need other people. He experienced loneliness as a young boy and reminds us that loneliness isn't just a condition of older people who live alone. It can impact all ages, both introverts and extroverts. Feeling lonely doesn't mean there is something wrong with us, but it can have serious health implications if ignored. In 2016, Dr. Murthy famously named loneliness the number-one public health problem in the country. It is amplified more now by a pandemic and shelter-in-place orders. If left unchecked, chronic loneliness has the same impact on the body as chronic stress. It increases our levels of inflammation in the body, which increases our risk of heart disease and other chronic illnesses. The solution to the loneliness epidemic is human connection in the form of relationships. It's the quality, not the quantity, of relationships that matter. Dr. Murthy encourages us to have relationships where we can show up honestly as ourselves because a chance to be real without the anxiety of crafting a false version of ourselves will help us feel deeply connected. His interviews with people across the country of all ages and backgrounds reveal a common feeling: a lack of belonging. People are craving a sense of being "home." He writes: "To be home is to be known. It is to be loved for who you are. It is to share a sense of common ground, common interests, pursuits, and values with others who truly care about you. In community after community, I met lonely people who felt homeless even though they had a roof over their heads." [1]

So, how do we build relationships in our third act? I tend to keep old friends close and, honestly, I've said more than once, "I don't need more friends." I see that statement is counter to the premise of this book, for if someone new enters my world and I am truly turning to God each day, I believe that "someone" deserves at least a greeting, a conversation, maybe a cup of coffee, and a listening ear. Who knows where it might lead?

Sometimes I find myself being self-serving when I reach out to new people, thinking about how they can enrich my life. A perfect example of this is five years ago when I accepted a German exchange student into our family during our youngest son's junior year in high school. It was so unlike me to make that kind of long-term commitment, but I was swayed when I learned the student was a tennis player. I was picturing him as a much-needed addition to our high school tennis team, and even imagined him helping our son's team win the conference championship. When he arrived, he admitted he wanted to play football instead! The joke was on me, but also the blessing. That was five years ago, and our German son, Tobi, and his parents are truly a special part of our family. God took my self-centered idea and turned it outward for the greater good.

I happen to be home alone all this week. I mention this simply because moments of solitude are, in fact, central to connecting to other people. We need that me-time to center ourselves. Therefore, this week, I'm trying to unplug a bit, take walks, and listen to my favorite music. It is truly a challenge for this curious extrovert. I haven't even turned on the television today! That might be due to finding and rereading parts of an old favorite book last evening. *Gift from the Sea*, written by Anne Morrow Lindbergh, is an intimate and honest conversation about "youth and age, love and marriage, solitude, peace, and contentment." Anne wrote the book while vacationing on Captiva Island in Florida in the early 1950s and uses imagery from the ocean as the canvas for her words. It is a true gift, one that I often give to new moms and those experiencing transition in their lives. Anne, wife of pioneer aviator Charles Lindbergh, has wise words to share about relationships, too. It is so beautiful that I honor her by sharing her words here:

"When you love someone, you do not love them all the time in exactly the same way from moment to moment. It is an impossibility. It is even a lie to pretend to. And yet this is exactly what most of us demand. We have so little faith in the ebb and flow of life, of love, of relationships. We leap at the flow of the tide and resist in terror its ebb. We are afraid it will never return. We insist on permanency, on duration, on continuity; when the only continuity possible, in life as in love, is in growth, in fluidity—in freedom."[2]

The key word here is *freedom.* To me, freedom to form meaningful relationships is reached through a daily exercise of turning to God with my emotional rocks that are weighing me down. They are stones of expectations, judgment, and fear. I know that God will take those stones and give me a lightness of being that will turn me towards others for the common good and the abundant life.

As a side note, Anne Lindbergh Morrow lived to be ninety-four.

Your Turn

1. Try to recall the last time you made a new friend. What prompted the relationship? Write a letter to that friend (don't worry, you don't have to send it if you don't want to). What would you say to them?

2. Did your view of loneliness change after reading this chapter? How?

3. Whose name popped into your head while reading this chapter? What steps could you take to connect with them? Think of one concrete way to reach out to one or more of these people in the next month and challenge yourself to follow through.

Chapter Seventeen

Stay Clever and Curious

"Which would you rather be if you had the choice—
divinely beautiful or dazzlingly clever or
angelically good?"
L.M. Montgomery, *Anne of Green Gables*

The meal that evening on our deck was a leisurely feast for our table of four, starting with wine and cheese, then a main course of delicate fish prepared in parchment paper, and a sunset dessert of fresh peach pie with homemade ice cream. Our friends—whom we had not hosted before—graciously thanked us as they headed out the door close to midnight. As we cleaned up the kitchen, Dan and I evaluated that the food turned out well; maybe the fish packets took too long, but all in all it was a good meal. The next morning, I woke up to a text from our guests: "Thank you so much for a perfect evening in which we could enjoy our friendship, great food and wine, and such engaging conversation!" As much as I love my cooking to be appreciated, I love even more for my words to matter. Hearing that our conversations were a highlight of the evening meant more than any adulations for my fish or pie. A simple meal of clever and curious conversation will be planned for our next gathering.

We all have measuring sticks that we use to see if we're up to par, if we've still got game, if we still are—for lack of a better word—*interesting*. You might be measuring yourself against others' daily lives as posted on social media. You know the sort of posts—weekends at the lake cabin, trips to national parks (including elevation and hiking successes), or birthday parties with grandchildren. I will admit that I do my share of sharing. I have a friend who recently messaged me after seeing my California road trip photos saying, "Love all your adventures and how you do life!" What a gracious response. I had to ask her how she has been able to avoid what Teddy Roosevelt meant when he said, "Comparison is the thief of joy." She quickly responded, "I always strive to be the best version of *me* and try my best to not compare that with someone else. My mission in life is to help others live their lives to the fullest and do the things that matter most to them. I've also really decided we are never done growing." Not surprising from my friend Kay. She is a retired nurse who now owns a couple of her own businesses. She is an inspiration for wholeness. Kay spent several months during the pandemic advocating for families whose loved ones are isolated in long-term care facilities. She was experiencing her own mother's isolation, and curiosity led her to collecting stories of others in the same situation. The result was a Facebook group that Kay created to highlight these stories and give a platform for conversations that eventually led to policy changes by connecting with state legislators.

Kay says her measuring stick is herself, but I'd say it's also how much she helps others live life to the fullest. In her words, "I am a curious person, and one of my all-time favorite pastimes is hearing people's stories and where they come from, what's their foundation, and what makes them tick. I find it fascinating." Kay and I have had some great coffee dates, and she brings her gift of listening each time. She says, "I like it to be a relaxed conversation, asking questions, and allowing people to be heard and not being the talker. People love that, and I love that; I feel this is where connections are made and lasting relationships formed."

Daniel Yankelovich, in his book *The Magic of Dialogue*, values conversation and brings clarity to what I experienced on our deck with our guests, and what Kay brings with her to the coffee shop. He says that dialogue is not conversation, discussion, or debate; rather, "it is seeking mutual understanding and harmony. We listen and respond to one another with an authenticity that forges a bond between us." [1] Have you experienced energy from talking with a friend, family member, or stranger when both of you are being curious and open? Be mindful of when those conversations occur. What words did you say? Did you spend more time listening intently? There might have been some cleverness tossed in, as well as some laughter. All good ingredients for meaningful dialogue. You may have even "hatched a plan," as my friend Jan and I like to say.

Laura Carstensen, director of the Stanford Center on Longevity, writes in *The Upside of Aging* about two "constellations" of goals that are universal to every stage of life, sometimes in competition. The first constellation is exploration and expanding horizons, and the second is emotional satisfaction and emotional meaning. [2] One could also call these constellations the "breadth" and "depth" of living. Dwell under these "stars" for a moment and think about your current goals or day-to-day life. Now consider which constellation your sights would turn to if your heart and ears are tuned into God. You may be called, like Kay, to dig deep into advocacy work, or you may hear the call of the Peace Corps, like my friend, Lon, whose story I shared earlier. You may not need to even step out of your house. Calling an old friend you haven't spoken to in years can yield dialogue that's meaningful for both of you. I wrote about this divine communication style in Chapter Five: by keeping your ears open to God's voice, rather than your own diminutive inner voice, you will freely turn to where you are needed most.

You may recall reading about my husband's recent retirement. We are now well into the fourth month of this new rhythm, and it has been a constant spiral, but neither down nor up—just lateral waves between "this is awesome" and "this is awful." Turn, turn, turn is a good visual here! Over the past three months, Dan applied for three positions in his field and was not offered jobs by any of them. I think his measuring stick snapped in half the day he learned this news. We analyzed the process and the interviews many times. One never exactly knows why a rejection happens, although it's hard to not wonder if his sixty-one birthdays were a factor. His self-care response was to retreat to the forest in our backyard, returning to the house to eat, sleep, and watch Hallmark movies. During the day, he is cutting out dead trees and trimming branches, and collecting firewood for the coming winter. He has also made plans to build a treehouse. A metaphor of out with the old and in with the new seems to be happening. He did announce to me last night that he thinks he won't be searching for a new job. He is ready to just maintain the interests and people and life we already have. The constellation he has set his sights on for now seems to be emotional satisfaction and emotional meaning. I'll happily be stargazing right by his side. He will continue to be clever and curious.

Carstensen, in *Upside*, tells all of us who are in our third act to not worry about using a measuring stick: "Age is associated with greater knowledge about the world, deeper expertise in selected domains, and concern for investing in activities and people that really matter." She adds, "It is critical that we do not overlook the real talent available in a resource never before available in human societies—aging minds."[2]

I look forward to rewriting this chapter in about ten years to see how God helped us live this time, these more days, for every purpose under Heaven.

Your Turn

1. Recall a recent dialogue that energized you. Did it change your relationship with that person?

2. Answer the question found in the book *Anne of Green Gables* quoted at the beginning of the chapter: "Which would you rather be if you had the choice—divinely beautiful or dazzlingly clever or angelically good?" Why?

3. The next time you're gathered with a group of friends or family, consider raising this question: How do you measure your life? Does your age sneak into that equation? Be bold and post these questions on your social media. Enjoy learning from the responses.

Chapter Eighteen

Generativity

"Could we with ink the ocean fill,
And were the skies of parchment made;
Were every stalk on earth a quill,
And every man a scribe by trade;
To write the love of God above
Would drain the ocean dry;
Nor could the scroll contain the whole,
Though stretched from sky to sky."
"The Love of God,"
Meir Ben Isaac Nehorai, 11th century

As I sit at my dining room table, which has been my writing
desk for several months now, I turn my gaze away from the piles

of books, sticky notes, and manuscripts to the two windows in front of me. October is, without a doubt, my favorite month. Out of one window is a stately red Autumn Blaze maple and a clump of elegant purple asters; out of the other window is a flickering golden birch tree leaning over copper-colored silver feather grass. All blowing in the South Dakota wind. The beauty is alarming. It is also a reminder that my birthday is near—October 22 is only two weeks away. Consequently, my goal of completing this book by my sixty-first birthday is also near. I am sounding the alarm to my brain, my intuition, and to my heart. It is as if I am nearing the tip of what I thought was an endless funnel of words that I wanted to share. In reality, the ones at the end of the funnel are the most stubborn to get out, but I will do my best.

The quote at the beginning of this chapter has been meaningful to me for years. It is the third verse of a hymn composed by Frederick M. Lehman in 1917. I first heard it when it was sung by my oldest son and his college choir at Augustana University. "The Love of God" was performed at a concert I attended while my father was living his last days on earth in the hospital nearby. Just typing these words now brings back all the emotions of hearing those beautiful lyrics for the first time. I included the verse in one of the daily emails to friends and family because the words perfectly described how my family and I felt about the boundless expressions of love and concern we were receiving from those who knew my dad. I remember researching the hymn and learning that the words used in the third verse were found handwritten on the wall of a patient's room in an insane asylum. They weren't discovered until the patient had died and was in his grave. The story goes that the words were written by the patient, Jewish poet Meir Ben Isaac Nehorai, in 1050 A.D.—an incredible and timeless gift to future generations. [1]

Caring for future generations is part of the work of aging. As a college student, I recall learning all the phases of psychological development established by Erik Erickson. I especially remember identifying with his late-teen phase of "identity versus confusion." Who and what was I supposed to be at age nineteen? It wasn't until 1982 (soon after I completed college) that Erickson named a phase for people forty-five to sixty-five as "generativity versus stagnation." It appears he reached the age of eighty and realized he was still developing, so the final phase, for those over sixty-five, he named "integrity versus despair." [2] These phases make sense to me and bring light to how I hope to live my third act of life.

Generativity is investing ourselves into forms of life and work that will outlive us. [2] Dr. George Vaillant, who shepherded the Harvard Study of Adult Development, a five-decade longitudinal study of Harvard medical students, learned that the basic rule of generativity is that biology flows downhill: "Parents should look after children" and "To be a generative parent enriches everyone." This affirms what I observed in my geriatric practice. Often adult children said they wanted to care for their aging parents in order to return the care that their parents had given to them. I would explain that this was not a fair exchange—caring for someone who is declining in function is different than caring for a child who is growing and flourishing. You choose to care for your aging parents because they need care, not because you are trying to pay them back. It also leaves open the door for someone else who might be more equipped to care for them. The Harvard study's lead researcher, George E. Valliant, M.D., in *Aging Well*, says: "We can give ourselves away only after ourselves are formed. Wheat must be ripened before it can make bread. Of course, as we reach middle life, we should help our parents help themselves. But we should help our parents out of gratitude and not at the cost of our own development." As Valliant suggests, the theory of generativity posits that people will become the best version of themselves to be ready to give themselves to the next generation, as opposed to its opposite, "stagnation," which means being static or stuck.

His Harvard study included curious questions. To me, one of the most intriguing was the question asked to participants when they turned sixty-five: "What have you learned from your children?" This turns the more expected question of "What did your children learn from you?" on its head. Findings revealed that the study participants who were aging most successfully were taking in what they had learned from their children and growing from those learnings in positive ways. I posed this question to Jan, one of my best friends. Admittedly she is only sixty, but she is the mother of three adult children. I have known her all my life, and it was a delight to hear her answers. She told me, "The first thing that comes to mind is something I've known for a long time. I've reminded myself of this so many times: 'My children are not me.' When Joel was in middle school, I realized he was not me and he was not my husband; Joel was HIMSELF. As individuals with their own path in life, their personalities come fully installed. This realization has made me more accepting of differences, and it has given me freedom as a parent to be more accepting and less judgmental. My sister puts it this way: 'Everyone brings something to the table.'"

The next essential step is to accept what is brought to the table and let it sit with you awhile. It might be new music, a new hobby, a new political opinion, a new dream. Let it all marinate within you and see what inspires you. As Vaillant reminds us, "Inspiration, after all, is a metaphor for how we take other people inside. Through our lungs, through our guts, and through our hearts." [2] Ultimately, the Harvard Study of Adult Development found a commonality of those who were aging most successfully: each was blessed with the gift that allowed the healing, hope, strength, and experience of others *inside*. I don't know the people in this Harvard study, but I know people who are like them. They are friends, neighbors, and family members who are open to the healing, hope, strength, and experiences of others. I have been watching them this past year. I see them assuming a posture of aging that turns their hearts towards others. Most of their time is spent not turning into themselves, but rather looking out and up to what new need or experience God might be putting in their path and saying yes!

As I watch the leaves through my dining room windows, I am impressed by the ongoing work of God's creation. This is a season of regeneration. Though we had our first killing frost last week in South Dakota, we still see evidence of life in a landscape that is making preparations for the cycle to begin again in the spring. My dad, a farmer, would have appreciated this warm, dry day to be out in the fields and harvesting the corn. He would have called it an "Indian summer." Many cultures around the world have a name for this fall gift of summertime. In Germany it is called *altweibersommer*, meaning "old women's summer." Aptly named? Well, I will take it as a reminder that this third act of life can be alarmingly beautiful and intentionally generous. Achingly, I also agree with the poet whose words I quoted at the beginning of the chapter, who realized that it is impossible to write the love of God. There is just too much of it. May we be inspired to share that love, our bounty, our experiences, and our hope with those who have yet to linger in the autumn of life. As Pete Seeger proclaimed when adding his own lyric to the Ecclesiastes text: "I swear it's not too late."

Your Turn

1. As moms, dads, aunts, uncles, or friends, what have you learned from the children in your life? Take time to write a letter or simply a text to those children thanking them for what they've taught you.

2. Recall a period of stagnation in your life. What got you unstuck? Or if you still feel stuck, what might your next steps be? Write down three actions and put them on your bathroom mirror to greet you each morning.

3. What would our world look like if everyone lived by the words, "I swear it's not too late"?

Chapter Nineteen

You Are Timeless

"Architecture is basically a container of something. I
hope they will enjoy not so much the teacup,
but the tea."
Yoshio Taniguchi

I awoke yesterday and caught a glimpse of my hand in front
of my face. With the Nashville winter sun pouring in through
the east window of our rented apartment, I was startled by
the fine lines and tiny brown spots that distinguished themselves in the bright light. *Whose hands are these?* I thought.
The shapes were familiar, and the long fingers wore two familiar rings—a small marquise diamond over forty years old on
the left and a silver band inset with a smooth blue stone on

the right. It was the skin that confused me. Its lines of weakened architecture seemed to blatantly confess my age. I'm glad I couldn't see my forehead. I bundled up in my warmest clothes fitting for an unusually cold and wintry Tennessee February and stepped outside for a walk. I tromped through the fresh snow in this quaint neighborhood, my favorite area of the city—12 South—for one reason: I wanted to look at the houses.

There were stately Victorians, angular Craftsmans (my favorite), and endearing bungalows. The only commonalities being the blanket of snow over each one and a timeless character that knit them all together. I'm sure most of them were close to a hundred years old. Their architecture confessed their age. What is it that draws us to these neighborhoods? For me there is endless variety—differently shaped roofs and configurations of windows, a range of porches from tiny to sprawling, and painted various colors from bright to dark. There is something inherently welcoming and mysteriously intriguing about each one. I am transported back to my childhood and want to ring the doorbell and say, "Trick or treat!" Stories seem to pour out of each door and rise from each chimney.

Back at the apartment, getting ready for my day, I glance at my sixty-something-year-old body in the bathroom mirror and am perplexed by what the passage of time has done to my own architecture. My body has given way to the effects of daily life, not unlike the homes in the 12 South neighborhood. As my husband observed of one house on a previous walk, "That's going to weather funny."

I wrote earlier about seeing ourselves as a whole being—body, mind, and spirit. This trio of God-created holy parts combine to get us out of bed each morning, inspire us to work, play, and serve our neighbor. Sometimes it will be the architecture of our hands that startles us, and other days it will be the architecture of our minds—stacking up arguments against our spouse or building a wall to conceal our feelings. It's been my experience that when my body is frustrating me or my mind is playing tricks on me, it is my *spirit*—my belief system, my faith—that lifts me out of myself. I then turn outward rather than inward. The fact that my skin is losing its elasticity and my mind is overwhelmed doesn't win the day. My faith frees me from focusing on the constraints of my body and mind and allows me to instead focus on others.

The body often seems to be the majority player in the body/mind/spirit dance. Do you recall discovering your first gray hair? My editor, Andrea, shared her account of recently discovering a silver strand in her gorgeous brunette hair (my adjective, not hers). She is a few years away from her thirtieth birthday and described the anxiety spiral that ensued until her husband came home, rolled his eyes, and said, "It's one hair, Andrea." At this time, no more have been found, but I'm sure they are being monitored.

I've heard aging described as being comfortable with the passage of time. I agree. I have loved each and every one of my birthdays and have insisted on celebrating them all. I have great friends who have made those wishes come true. My fiftieth birthday party was commandeered by my dear friends Jana and Kirsten. They love a theme party and knew of my lifelong regret of never owning a Barbie. (Side note: My sister, Patty, had a Barbie doll, sister Cindy had a Midge—with the flipped red hair—and I had a Tammy doll, which never seemed quite as good. However, I just googled her and discovered she is now worth $113!) It just so happens that Barbie and I are the same age; she was also created in 1959. So, my friends planned the perfect surprise party—I arrived and was whisked away to the bedroom to receive a Barbie makeover, consisting of lots of make-up, poofy hair, orange and pink sixties' dress, and white go-go boots. My dream came true when all the guests each gifted me a different Barbie doll. What a delight to open each one, take photos, and then pack them up to be shared with a local orphanage. A fiftieth birthday—or even a thirtieth or fortieth—can be startling in a good way or a bad way. Let your spirit lead you.

While in Nashville, I had the delight of interviewing three women who are current clients of another of our small business endeavors, Profile®—a healthy weight loss program. By far the most satisfying part of this small business is listening to the stories of our clients. They seem to just pour out (not unlike the stories from the houses of the 12 South neighborhood). A major part of the program is individualized weekly coaching sessions with one of our trained coaches. I had the opportunity to visit with three women who met each other at a local prayer group and encouraged each other in this new health journey. I asked each of them my favorite geriatric nurse question: "How old would you be if you didn't know how old you were?" (This question was first posed by legendary baseball player, Satchel Paige, [1] who played all of his big-league games after turning forty-two. His pithy question has the power to reveal so much about one's current state of body, mind, and spirit.) I presented this question to this group of three friends. Collectively, they had lost 181 pounds over the past year, yet throughout the interview, it was evident that their transformations went way beyond the change in their body architecture and seeped deeply into their mind and spirit. Sheila, sixty-eight, an articulate recent retiree and widow, quickly answered, "Forty! I feel great, and I know I move faster than some young people sometimes!" Dabne, an effervescent seventy-seven-year-old responded, "Thirty-five! In fact, I never felt this good at thirty-five. I have never been without pain until now. I have had pain in my legs my whole life. I had back surgery eighteen months ago, and I'm so grateful this program has forced me to walk. I can walk the 1.6 miles down and back up my street every day now. I never believed I could, because I couldn't. This has been the greatest freedom. I am so thankful. I am in awe. I'm surprised that I would feel so good. I thought being tired was being equated with old age ... and, my God, it's not!" Kathyrn, an insightful and competitive woman in her late sixties, followed with, "I feel late twenties or thirty. I look in the mirror and say that's who I really am—the athlete that I was in my twenties."

It was such a naturally open yet mysteriously intriguing conversation with these three women—not unlike my walk through the neighborhood of houses in 12 South. This community of friends seem unaffected by the passage of time. Three very different personalities and architectures knit together by the faith they share and the blanket of Christ's love and forgiveness. Timeless promises create timeless lives.

Your Turn

1. Describe a neighborhood where you like to walk or drive. What is it that attracts you?

2. Sketch a house that looks like you feel right now. If you're more comfortable using words, describe how each part of the house looks, including the windows, front door, the roof, the front yard, the backyard.

3. What would you tell your twenty-something self about aging? What preparations should you make? What words would calm you about aging? Would you use the word "aging" or something softer, like "passage of time"?

Chapter Twenty

Be a Mountain Goat

"Never bend your head. Always hold it high. Look the
world straight in the face."
Helen Keller

The roads through my home state of South Dakota are capti-
vating. On the eastern side of the state there is a patchwork of
fields of corn and beans, and one sees pastures of cattle, barn-
yards of pigs, power lines of blackbirds, and deer in the ditches.
At the westernmost side of the state are our beloved Badlands
and Black Hills. The roads spiral through the moonscape of the
Badlands with their pink and mustard colored rock formations
with sharp peaks, passing an occasional Big Horn sheep and
the playgrounds of prairie dogs. On the intimate drive through

the pine forests and meadows of our Black Hills, everyone's eyes are peeled for the next wooly bison or skittish elk. I recall one particularly memorable drive, as we approached the final curves toward Mt. Rushmore, we made a turn while circling Horse Thief Lake and spotted three white furry mountain goats perched on the granite mountain wall high above the small lake. They appeared to be almost flat against the wall—from our view we couldn't see any path on which they could stand. It was as if someone were mysteriously holding those mountain goats with some invisible strings. I imagined the puppet scene from the *Sound of Music*, where the Von Trapp children were singing, "High on a hill was a lonely goatherd." Their confidence and sure footing on rocky terrain was enviable.

Mountain goats have become my newest spirit animal. I still love dogs and butterflies, but as I learn about mountain goats and their ability to traverse any challenge, I'm thinking about getting a stuffed toy one to carry around for daily inspiration. My research on mountain goats led me to a fascinating book: *A Beast the Color of Winter: The Mountain Goat Observed*.[1] The author and researcher Douglas H. Chadwick revealed the following facts—some fun, some phenomenal.

- They can withstand temperatures as low as 51 degrees below zero and winds up to 99 mph.
- They spend most of their time grazing.
- Their babies are 6.6 pounds and attempt to run and climb within hours of birth.
- The mothers position themselves below their kids on steep slopes to stop free falls.

- Their lifespans are limited by the wearing down of their teeth.

- Their powerful shoulders and neck muscles help propel them up steep slopes.

- Their hoofs are designed like suction cups to traverse narrow ledges only inches wide.

- The pupils of their eyes are shaped like rectangles, maximizing their peripheral vision.

- Mountain goats have an amazing ability to find something to cling to.

I was inspired by all these findings, but I was transfixed when I discovered that last one. It's an incredible image. This ancient breed has survived over eight million years, avoiding predators and scavenging for food by *finding something to cling to*. Watching them cling to the rocky cliffs near Horse Thief Lake was a demonstration in confidence. Their steps appeared carefree without being reckless; intentional yet ready to turn at any moment. Somehow, they knew they were being held to the earth.

In a previous chapter, I shared the theologian Steven Paulson's comparison of faith to drops of water clinging to the outside of a water pitcher on a hot summer day. [2] We cling to the voice of Christ. I now have another image for faith, one that speaks to the passage of time and finding our way through the ups and downs of life. Who of us hasn't compared our current situation in life to a mountain climb or unknown terrain or uncertainty of where to go next? Sometimes we're just stuck and let others pull our strings, like the Von Trapp children did for their Lonely Goatherd puppets. By clinging to our faith, we have confidence that God will direct our steps. By hearing the Gospel—Christ's words of forgiveness—we are gifted a freedom and grace that will release us each day to move about intentionally yet nimbly. We may not know today what turn our life will take tomorrow, but we can be confident in clinging to the One to make that turn. Are you feeling your inner mountain goat yet?

It's reasonable that you may be feeling more like Habakkuk, the Old Testament prophet, whose short three-chapter book begins with a very clear complaint to God: "How long, Lord, must I call for help, but you do not listen? Or cry out to you, 'Violence!' but you do not save? Why do you make me look at injustice? Why do you tolerate wrongdoing? Destruction and violence are before me; there is strife, and conflict abounds." (Habakkuk 1: 2–3)

These words, written around 600 B.C., could have easily been written today. Habakkuk spoke these words on behalf of a people who were fearful of the evil that surrounded them and frustrated that God seemed inactive in their lives. After hearing Habakkuk's plea, God revealed his plan to him—to bring peace to His people. Not in the way that they expected, but in the way that he planned. It arrived through the Babylonians, who had been their enemies but were transformed by God for a new purpose to build God's kingdom. Habakkuk responded with these words of praise, "The Sovereign Lord is my strength; he makes my feet like the feet of a deer, he enables me to tread on the heights." (Habakkuk 3:19)

These are words to cling to. The apostle Paul writes in his letter to the Romans in the New Testament: "So, faith comes from hearing the Good News. And people hear the Good News when someone tells them about Christ." (Romans 10:17, New Century Version.) The Good News is that Christ takes our sins from us. We confess, hand them over, and in exchange he gives us new life each day—a new life to live in faith, freedom, and confidence with the Holy Spirit as our guide. Mysteriously, we are sure-footed on all the rough and high places. There is nothing for us to give God in return. We only need to cling to Him in belief, like the Mountain Goat clings to the mountain. It brings to mind what my wise professor friend, Dr. Ken Jones, who commented earlier in this book on grief, recently wrote in the closing of his book, *A Lutheran Toolkit*: "That's what our Lord has been after all along. To be bound to you so tightly that you can't spot where Jesus ends and you begin. To bind you to your neighbor so tightly that you're compelled to serve." [3]

I had a wise mentor early in my nursing career who asked me a powerful question when I was contemplating a job change at age twenty-four. She looked at me and simply said, "How big a playground do you want?" I have repeated that question to myself many times throughout my life as new opportunities arise or when life feels stagnant. The depth and breadth of my playgrounds through the years have made for an interesting life, for which I am grateful.

As I move on to my next birthday, and the one after that, and the one after that, I am going to ask myself, "How big a playground do I want?" I will ask while clinging to Christ. I will open my ears to hear God's word. God's word will block out my own voice of self-talk and will tune me into the voice of my neighbor. The playground might be tiny and in the confines of my home as I live with my still-retired husband. It will stretch a bit bigger when I sit in my girlfriend's kitchen as she grieves her brother's illness. The playground may someday contain the biggest mountain I've ever had to climb or the greenest valley I've ever seen with a full moon to dance beneath. Whatever the setting, I will bravely bring my inner mountain goat to traverse all the ruts and realities. I will look the world straight in the face. There is no time to be afraid and one very incredible view waiting for all of us. Let's pass the time together.

Your Turn

I invite you to write the questions for this last chapter. What are you curious about? What are you questioning about the how/when/where/why of your next decade? Consider this quote from one of my favorite books, *A More Beautiful Question: The Power of Inquiry to Spark Breakthrough Ideas* by Warren Berger: "A beautiful question is an ambitious yet actionable question that can begin to shift the way we perceive or think about something—and that might serve as a catalyst to bring about change."[4] An example would be the playground question, but there is no need to limit your questions to this chapter. Turn back the pages of this book or simply search your heart. Write an ambitious question (or three) that moves you to act. It may propel you to further research a certain topic or enter into a dialogue with others. God loves hearing your beautiful questions, too. There may be a question that you have been hiding inside you all your life. Now is the time to write it down and let it spur your curiosity and your confidence to find the answer and move to action.

1.

2.

3.

Commencement

Who doesn't recall their high school graduation ceremony?
Mine was in the tidy but tiny Hurley City Park, one block
square; my grandparents' house was across the street. That
Sunday afternoon, my twenty-one classmates and I processed
along to our high school band's playing of "Pomp and Circum-
stance." Although our school colors were orange and black,
we wore our chosen class colors—the boys in dark blue gowns
and the girls in light blue. The girls' feathered bangs, inspired
by actress Farrah Fawcett, confidently peaked out from under
their mortar boards. The boys were happy to hide their fresh
haircuts under their graduation caps. It was 1977 and it was
our commencement day. Each of my classmates was looking
forward to their future with a mix of hope, fear, uncertainty,
and excitement. As I write this closing chapter, I see it more as
a "commencement" than a "conclusion."

At the beginning of this book, I asked us to collaborate on what our sixties and seventies could look like. I acknowledged that we may end up with more questions than answers, and I hope you wrote some of both in the margins. My dream is that those notes turn into conversations with others. The topic of aging shouldn't be avoided; it should be embraced. Marc Freedman asks an important question in the book *The Upside of Aging*: "So, how do we turn this nascent and still murky stage of life from one that is all too often characterized by identity void, economic disengagement, and societal confusion into one that has a shot at being the new crown of life?" [1] The play on words here is too easy for me. I need to remind myself daily that I wear a crown that was given to me at my baptism. I am a child of God, a kid of the kingdom, no matter what age I am. I am a part of the royal priesthood of believers. Where does that reminder come from? It comes from what I put in my ears each morning—the word of God. It magically and mysteriously drowns out my own voice of self-preservation, self-pity, judgment, or fear. Words like this from Romans Chapter 5: 1–5:

"Therefore, since we have been justified through faith, we have peace with God through our Lord Jesus Christ, through whom we have gained access by faith into this grace in which we now stand. And we boast in the hope of the glory of God. Not only so, but we also glory in our sufferings, because we know that suffering produces perseverance; perseverance, character; and character, hope. And hope does not put us to shame, because God's love has been poured out into our hearts through the Holy Spirit, who has been given to us."

Words like "peace," "faith," "grace," "hope," and "perseverance" inform my everyday life, freeing me from society's expectations of what a third act of life should look like and allow me to turn to God's imaginative, serendipitous, and abundant plan for my life. To repeat Pastor Martin Marty's words: "What we plan for is not as satisfying as what comes by chance and through divine generosity." [2]

I am excited for the magic and mystery of more days, and I hope you are, too. Let's hydrate with a big glass of water, straighten our crowns, grab our purple crayons and our stuffed mountain goats and begin a transforming dialogue together. With our ears open to God, we will usher in a new version of the third act of life. It's our turn.

Suggestions for Using *Turning* with a Group

I invite you to share this book in a group setting, whether your group is faith-based or secular; discussions will flow either way. Don't let the length of the book dissuade you from engaging in-depth dialogue; the "Your Turn" section at the end of each chapter should lead to good discussion. However, here are some additional ideas for building on the themes in *Turning* that should lead to rich discussions, new learnings, deepened relationships, and the always essential ingredient: fun!

Open the gathering with a backdrop of music from any decade, vintage candies, or by sharing tastes of a beloved family recipe.

If your group is faith focused, you could assign opening devotions that feature a character from the Bible who does remarkable things in his or her older years, such as Naomi, Elizabeth, Anna, and Simeon.

Your first session might focus on hearing about each person's role model for aging. Invite the participants to bring a photo or memento of that person. Find common themes and surprising differences.

In the physical health sections of the book, you can branch off into other areas besides the ones covered in the book. Encourage people to share their personal stories if they are comfortable doing so. Add a sensory experience to your post-discussion refreshments, such as wine tasting, herbal tea tasting, or a variety of cheeses or chocolates.

Bring magazines and scissors for the discussion on culture. Make an inspiration board for aging, or even an anti-inspiration board exploring what today's news and advertising tells the world about the experience of aging.

When discussing retirement or taking a gap year, have each person make a vision board, either prior to the group discussion or at the gathering. There are apps available for digital vision boards or bring out the scissors and magazines again!

Bring in some flowering plants for the Chapter Fourteen discussion on "Flowers and Wild Forgiveness." Consider meeting near a flower garden at a local park to inspire discussion.

For the daily bread discussion in Chapter Fifteen, invite participants to bring a loaf of bread to exchange with others in the group or collect loaves to deliver to the local food pantry.

When discussing loneliness, you may want to invite a local social worker, police officer, pastor, or public health nurse to comment on their observations of loneliness in your community.

Use film clips to stimulate discussion around any of the book topics. Check out *Grumpy Old Men, Driving Miss Daisy, The Curious Case of Benjamin Button, The Trip to Bountiful, The Age of Adaline,* and *Wild Strawberries.*

Endnotes

Chapter 1: Let's Begin Together

1. Seeger, Pete. "Turn, Turn, Turn." First published as "To Everything There Is a Season" performed on the Limelighters' album *Folk Matinee.* RCA Victor, 1962.

2. The Seekers, "Turn, Turn, Turn." YouTube, *The Seekers Down Under* 1966/6 youtu.be/VRg9NkIdjVs.

3. Pelikan, Jaroslav, and Hilton C. Oswald, editors. *Luther's Works.* Saint Louis: Concordia, 1972. p. 50.

4. Pelikan, Jaroslav, and Hilton C. Oswald, editors. *Luther's Works.* Saint Louis: Concordia, 1972. p. 52.

Chapter 2: **Where Did You Learn to Age?**

1. Presenter Pastor Charlotte Gambill. (October 4, 2020) Dare to Be Conference online.

2. Quotation from *An Inland Voyage, The Works of Robert Louis Stevenson*, Swanston edn, Vol. i. London: Chatto and Windus, 1911.

3. Weaver, Frances. *The Girls with the Grandmother Faces: A Celebration of Life's Potential for Those Over 55*. New York: Hyperion, 1996.

Chapter 3: **Culture**

1. Ogburn, William F. *Social Change with Respect to Culture and Original Nature*. New York: B.W. Huebsch, Inc., 1922.

2. Dychtwald, Ken. "A Longevity Market Emerges." *The Upside of Aging: How Long Life Is Changing the World of Health, Work, Innovation, Policy, and Purpose*. Edited by Paul H. Irving and Rita Beamish. Hoboken, New Jersey: John Wiley & Sons, Inc., 2014.

3. Vaynerchuk, Gary. "Ask Gary Vee" podcast from @GaryVee, Instagram, August 10, 2019.

4. Bregman, Peter. "A Good Way to Change a Corporate Culture." *Harvard Business Review*. June 25, 2009, hbr. org/2009/06/the-best-way-to-change-a-corpo.html

5. Freedman, Marc. "Encore: Mapping the Route to Second Acts." *The Upside of Aging: How Long Life Is Changing the World of Health, Work, Innovation, Policy, and Purpose.* Edited by Paul H. Irving and Rita Beamish. Hoboken, New Jersey: John Wiley & Sons, Inc., 2014.

6. Carstensen, Laura L. "Our Aging Population—It May Just Save Us All." *The Upside of Aging: How Long Life Is Changing the World of Health, Work, Innovation, Policy, and Purpose.* Edited by Paul H. Irving and Rita Beamish. Hoboken, New Jersey: John Wiley & Sons, Inc., 2014.

Chapter 4: Activity vs. Rest

1. Kaling, Mindy. *Is Everyone Hanging Out Without Me? (And Other Concerns)*, p.5. New York City: Three Rivers Press, 2011.

2. Katzmarzyk, et al. "Sitting Time and Mortality from All Causes, Cardiovascular Disease, and Cancer." *Medicine & Science in Sports & Exercise*, 2009, p. 998–1005.

3. "A Lifetime of Regular Exercise Slows down Ageing, Study Finds." *News Centre*, King's College London, March 8, 2018. https://www.kcl.ac.uk/news/a-lifetime-of-regular-exercise-slows-down-ageing-study-finds-1.

4. Department of Health and Human Services USA. *Physical Activity Guidelines for Americans. 2nd Ed.*, 2018

5. Swiger, Devra. "How Pilates Makes You Ageless." *Pilates Bridge: Connecting the Pilates Community*, http://pilatesbridge. com/ageless. Accessed October 10, 2020.

Chapter 5: The Power of a Scoop of Water

1. Rodgers & Hammerstein's *Cinderella,* directed by Charles S. Dubin. Samuel Golden, 1965. www.youtube.com/ watch?v=4xkQjuwihYl

2. Evangelical Lutheran Church in America. *Supplemental Resources for Use within the Evangelical Lutheran Worship Service of Marriage.* Minneapolis: Augsburg Fortress, 2016.

3. McIntosh, James. "Fifteen Benefits of Drinking Water." *Medical News Today*, July 16, 2018, www.medicalnewstoday. com/articles/290814

4. O'Toole, Garson. "I Know of a Cure for Everything: Salt Water ... Sweat, or Tears, or the Salt Sea. *Quote Investigator*. Quoteinvestigator.com.

Dinesen, Isak. Introduction by Dorothy Canfield. Quote from "The Deluge at Norderney," featured in *Seven Gothic Tales by Isak Dinesen*, page 39. Harrison Smith and Robert Haas, New York, 1934.

5. "ELCA Service of Holy Baptism" (paraphrased)*, Lutheran Book of Worship*, p. 121. Minneapolis: Augsburg Fortress, 1978.

6. Jones, Ken Sundet. *A Lutheran Toolkit*, p. 73. Irvine, California: 1517 Publishing, 2020.

Chapter 6: Do You Hear What I Hear?

1. Searchfield, Grant D., et al. "Are Hearing Aids the Answer? Hearing Loss, Reducing Tinnitus Perception, and Slowing Cognitive Decline." *Tinnitus Today*, vol. 44, no. 1, Spring 2019, pp. 17–20.

2. Dawes P, Emsley R, Cruickshanks KJ, Moore DR, Fortnum H, Edmondson-Jones M, et al. (2015) "Hearing Loss and Cognition: The Role of Hearing Aids, Social Isolation and Depression." *PLoS ONE* 10[3]: e0119616. doi:10.1371/journal. pp. 1–10.

Chapter 7: Ears Open and Head Up

1. Paulson, Steven. *Luther for Armchair Theologians*. Louisville, Kentucky: Westminster John Knox Press, 2004.

2. Luther, Martin. *Luther's Works, Volume 25: Lectures on Romans, Glosses and Schoilia (Luther's Works)*, p. 345, see also pp. 291–92. Saint Louis: Concordia, 1972.

Chapter 8: The Wonder Years

1. *The Wonder Years* created by Carol Black, Neal Marlens, pilot episode, season 1, episode 1, 1988, www.dailymotion.com/video/x5v8lff

2. Niles, John Jacob. *I Wonder as I Wander.* Originally published in *Songs of the Hill Folk* in 1934. www.godtube.com/popular-hymns/i-wonder-as-i-wander/

Chapter 9: Fear or Trust

1. Marty, Martin E. *Speaking of Trust: Conversing with Luther about the Sermon on the Mount.* Minneapolis: Augsburg Fortress, 2003.

Chapter 10: Invisible

1. Paul, Dr. Margaret. "I Used to Feel Invisible to Others Until I Did These 4 Things." *Mind, Body, Green, Mindfulness.* Updated January 26, 2021. www.mindbodygreen.com/0-15081/4-ways-youre-making-yourself-invisible-to-others.

2. Johnson, Nicole. *The Invisible Woman: When Only God Sees.* Nashville: Thomas Nelson, 2005.

Chapter 11: Let Yourself Be Surprised!

1. Bridges, William. *Transitions: Making Sense of Life's Changes.* pp 78–82. Cambridge: Massachusetts, 2004.

2. Pizzo, Philip A. "New Transitions: A Changing Journey of Life and Health." *The Upside of Aging: How Long Life Is Changing the World of Health, Work, Innovation, Policy, and Purpose.* Edited by Paul H. Irving and Rita Beamish, p. 226. Hoboken, New Jersey: John Wiley & Sons, Inc., 2014.

Chapter 12: **Grief and Loss**

1. Gwin, Connor. "The Ubiquity of Grief (and How I Tried to Climb the Ladder)." *Mockingbird*, June 8, 2016. https://mbird.com/2016/06/the-ubiquity-of-grief-and-how-i-tried-to-climb-the-ladder/.

2. Callanan, Maggie and Patricia Kelley. *Final Gifts*. New York: Simon & Schuster, Inc. 1992.

Chapter 13: **Sketching Joy**

1. Johnson, Crockett. *Harold and the Purple Crayon*. New York: HarperCollins Publishers, 1955.

2. Klee, Paul. Paul Klee *Paintings, Biography, and Quotes*, www.paulklee.net/paul-klee-quotes.jsp

Chapter 14: **Flowers and Wild Forgiveness**

1. Paulson, Steven. "The Most Important Reformation Text in All of Scripture." Audio Blog Post. Scripture First. Luther House, January 20, 2020.

Chapter 15: **Daily Bread and Butter**

1. Croghan, Chris. "What Is Daily Bread?" Audio Blog Post. Scripture First. Luther House, July 27, 2020.

Chapter 16: **Relationships**

1. Murthy, Vivek H. *Together: The Healing Power of Human Connection in a Sometimes Lonely World.* New York: Harper-Collins, 2020.

2. Lindbergh, Ann Morrow. *Gift from the Sea.* New York: Pantheon, 1955.

Chapter 17: **Stay Clever and Curious**

1. Yankelovich, Daniel. *The Magic of Dialogue: Transforming Conflict into Cooperation.* New York: Touchstone, 2001.

2. Carstensen, Laura L. "Our Aging Population—It May Just Save Us All." Quoted from p. 3 of *The Upside of Aging: How Long Life Is Changing the World of Health, Work, Innovation, Policy, and Purpose.* Edited by Paul H. Irving and Rita Beamish. Hoboken, New Jersey: John Wiley & Sons, Inc., 2014.

Chapter 18: **Generativity**

1. "Music of the Message: The Story of 'The Love of God,'" *Ministry International Journal for Pastors.* Archives September 1950. www.ministrymagazine.org/archive/1950/09/the-story-of-the-love-of-god.

2. Vaillant, George E. *Aging Well.* New York: Little, Brown, and Company, 2003.

Chapter 19: You're Timeless

1. "Satchel Page Quotes." Baseball Almanac. www.baseball-almanac.com/quotes/.

Chapter 20: Be a Mountain Goat

1. Chadwick, Douglas H. *A Beast the Color of Winter: The Mountain Goat Observed.* Lincoln, Nebraska, 1983.

2. Paulson, Steven. *Luther for Armchair Theologians.* Louisville, Kentucky: Westminster John Knox Press, 2004.

3. Jones, Ken Sundet. *A Lutheran Toolkit.* Irvine, California: 1517 Publishing, 2020.

4. Berger, Warren. *A More Beautiful Question: The Power of Inquiry to Spark Breakthrough Ideas.* New York: Bloomsbury, 2014.

Commencement

1. Freedman, Marc. "Encore: Mapping the Route to Second Acts." *The Upside of Aging: How Long Life Is Changing the World of Health, Work, Innovation, Policy, and Purpose.* Edited by Paul H. Irving and Rita Beamish. Hoboken, New Jersey: John Wiley & Sons, Inc., 2014.

2. Marty, Martin E. *Speaking of Trust: Conversing with Luther about the Sermon on the Mount.* Minneapolis: Augsburg Fortress, 2003.

Acknowledgments

Thank you to:

My husband, Dan, and our four children and their significant others—Ian and Paige, Julia and Luke, Elliot and Kara, and Mason and Ellie. They deserve matching cheerleading sweaters and some strawberry pie.

My dad, who often said, "Can't never done nothin,'" and to my mom, whose last handwritten words to me were, "Do all you can to be someone or learn something." Those words have fed me for years.

The friends and strangers whose stories illuminated the topics of this book—thank you for helping me connect the dots.

Andrea Van Essen, whose good taste and creativity elevated all things related to my book. She reminds me of a younger me, only with better editing skills and a cuter puppy.

Joyce Kaatz, my forever nurse colleague, who delivered

encouragement at just the right time and held impromptu focus groups around her kitchen table when I couldn't decide stuff.

Jan Brue Enright—my longest friend, librarian, and bookworm—whose opinion on anything I will value till the end of my days.

My early readers: Ali, Ashley, Chris, Joyce, Jan, Katie, Ken, Pat, Margo, Mary, Sarah, Steve, and Tanya, whose reflections challenged me and gave me confidence to keep writing.

The staff at the Luther House of Study and 1517, whose teachings fueled my desire to write a book that looks at aging through a theological lens.

My friends at the C-Suite Network, who role-modeled writing a book as a realistic endeavor—and fun to boot.

To all the '60s and '70s musical artists whose tunes kept me going. Check out my playlist on my website beckybluewrites.com.

Turn it up, and turn the page.